THE CLOSET CULTIVATOR

by

ED ROSENTHAL

LAST GASP
OF SAN FRANCISCO

The first days are the hardest days, don't you worry any more
When life looks like Easy Street, there is danger at your door
Think this through with me, let me know your mind
What I want to know is, Are you kind?

It's a buck-dancer's choice my friend
Better take my advice
You know all the rules by now
And the fire from the ice . . .

From "Uncle John's Band" by Robert Hunter, The Grateful Dead. Courtesy Robert Hunter

This book is dedicated to the Scythians, who knew how to get high, even if they did not have a pipe or papers.

Photographs by Ed Rosenthal. Photographs were taken on location using either an Olympus OM2 camera with Zuiko lenses or a Contax camera with Zeiss lenses. Most film exposures were Kodachrome 64 or 200 ASA. Photographs on pages 79, 89, 90, 91, 97 and 110 by T.L. with a Pentax ME Super using Pentax lenses.

Cover Drawing: Pauline Phung
Cover Design: Jane Klein
Cover Type: Pam Wilson
Book Design: Baba Ron Turner
Illustrations: Larry Todd
Typography: BookPrep

Published by: Last Gasp of San Francisco
P.O. Box 410067
San Francisco, CA 94141-0067

ISBN 0-86719-359-X

First Printing June 1991 10 11 12 98 97

Printed in Hong Kong

CONTENTS

FOREWORD

This has been the hardest book for me to write because knowledge about growing marijuana has been increasing at a geometric rate. Just as one method of cultivation has reached the apex of efficiency, totally new technologies enter the picture. The new methods offer significant advantages and will probably eclipse the old systems in popularity. My publisher patiently waited while I tried to solve my dilemma. I didn't want to write a book about a dinosaur, and I did not have enough hard information about the new developments.

As the deadlines came and went I still contemplated my dilemma. Then one evening, while attending a Grateful Dead concert, I saw how to precipitate the information. In this book I finally let my hair down. I have tried to detail information about "closet cultivation" in an informal way; to explain the madness behind the method. I hope that you find the book interesting, informative and inspiring.

PREFACE

Cannabis was one of the first plants cultivated by humans. Its fibers and seeds have been found in excavations of sites of human communities that are over 6000 years old. The plant has many uses and helped societies advance time and time again.

The symbiotic relationship humans have had with cannabis probably began when a hunter-gatherer discovered the plant's seed-laden branches. The seeds are still used as a grain and are easily gathered from varieties which hold them on the colas (branches laden with buds).

The fiber sheath around the stem is one of the strongest and longest fibers in the plant world. It is easily removed from the core after it has been retted, or left to soak for a while. The fiber was probably discovered after lying in a pool or puddle. Hemp fiber allowed many human communities to make their first rope and netting (both revolutionary developments) and then to make the move from animal hides to plant fiber clothing.

Humans discovered the psychoactive qualities of the plant thousands of years ago. The Scythians, who lived in northeastern Europe around 100 B.C., inhaled cannabis fumes in enclosed rooms. The practices were described by Herodotus, a Roman, who is considered by Westerners to be the world's first historian. The tribe had not yet discovered the efficiencies of the smoking pipe.

Before recorded history, various cannabis varieties were developed by a combination of selective breeding and acclimatization. For instance, people gathering seeds for food would tend to propagate large-seeded plants whose seeds stayed on the stem.

Cannabis usually developed into hemp in areas above the 30th parallel and contained small but variable amounts of the psychoactive substance, THC. Hemp does contain large amounts of a nearly non-psychoactive precursor of THC, cannabidiol, or CBD. The ratio of CBD to THC in cannabis increases with increasing latitudes of adapted plants.

A very hardy semi-weedy variety of cannabis, ruderalis, is found in the northern Steppes and is still used as a animal food grain. This variety also has a variable amount of THC.

Marijuana can be defined as the varieties of the cannabis plant cultivated for the psychoactive substance THC and its analogs. Marijuana is one of the most widely distributed plants in the world. It is grown in every county of the United States. Traditionally it has been grown in areas from the 30th parallel N to the Equator and then to the 30th parallel S. Since the 1960's it's range has been increased to the 60th parallel.

Marijuana and hemp are varieties of the same species cannabis, and are sometimes interbred to develop new varieties. Most of the chemical and morphological differences and the extremely diverse gene-pool are artifacts of cannabis's symbiotic relationship with humans. Humans carried seeds all over the world, and bred the plant to meet particular needs. This process continues today.

Modern marijuana growers are following in a great tradition. The plant has been re-discovered many times for one of its products after having been forgotten by previous generations. Americans are growing the plant today only for its psychoactive qualities. However, there are several reasons to think that when the prohibitions against its use are eliminated, the hemp plant will also be grown commercially in the U.S.

Cannabis fiber is not only the longest and one of the strongest in the plant kingdom, but depending on the variety, methods of cultivation, curing and processing, the fiber can be used for anything from ship rope to the finest linen-like material. Virtually no scientific experimentation has been done on modifying the fiber for various uses. Yet in countries where its cultivation is permitted, including France, Italy, and Yugoslavia, it is one of the most profitable crops grown. In these countries hemp is grown primarily for its fiber, which is used to make paper including very high quality non-deteriorating stock.

Cannabis pulp could be used in bio-mass operations, for paper making, and as a substitute ingredient in place of wood fiber. It would be much more profitable to use cannabis rather than softwood for by-products. Since cannabis takes only one season to grow, farmers could better adjust plans according to market conditions. Cannabis actually yields more mass per acre than most forests.

Cannabis seed can be used as a high protein animal feed and also for its oil, which has many industrial uses. A high protein animal feed can be made from the mash after it is pressed for its oil.

Cannabis is still intimately involved in a symbiotic relationship with humans. This special relationship will help both species evolve and will continue to alter both of their destinities.

Chapter 1
THE THEORY

The most important factor in producing high yielding, potent marijuana is the plant's genes. The goal of the grower is to cultivate a garden of healthy, vigorous, fast-growing plants which are induced to flower while they are still short. Indoor marijuana farms are limited spaces. To succeed they must be used as efficiently as possible.

To get the highest yield gardeners grow many small plants rather than a few large ones. Smaller plants yield more per square foot of space, mature faster, and are easier to care for than large ones. People used to think that size or age were important, but they soon found out that maturity or ripeness is the important factor. As the buds on the plant ripen, their potency increases. Depending on how intensive the technique and the variety being grown, plants are forced to flower when they are between 8-15 inches tall. Mature plants reach a height of 18-30 inches.

Plants forced when they are small have little chance to develop side shoots. This means that each plant uses not only a smaller vertical space, but has a smaller radius. Plants which are flowered when they are very small can be placed very close together. Short plants use much less vertical space so gardeners often find it convenient to divide the growing area into several levels of shelves or bunks. See illustration on page 2.

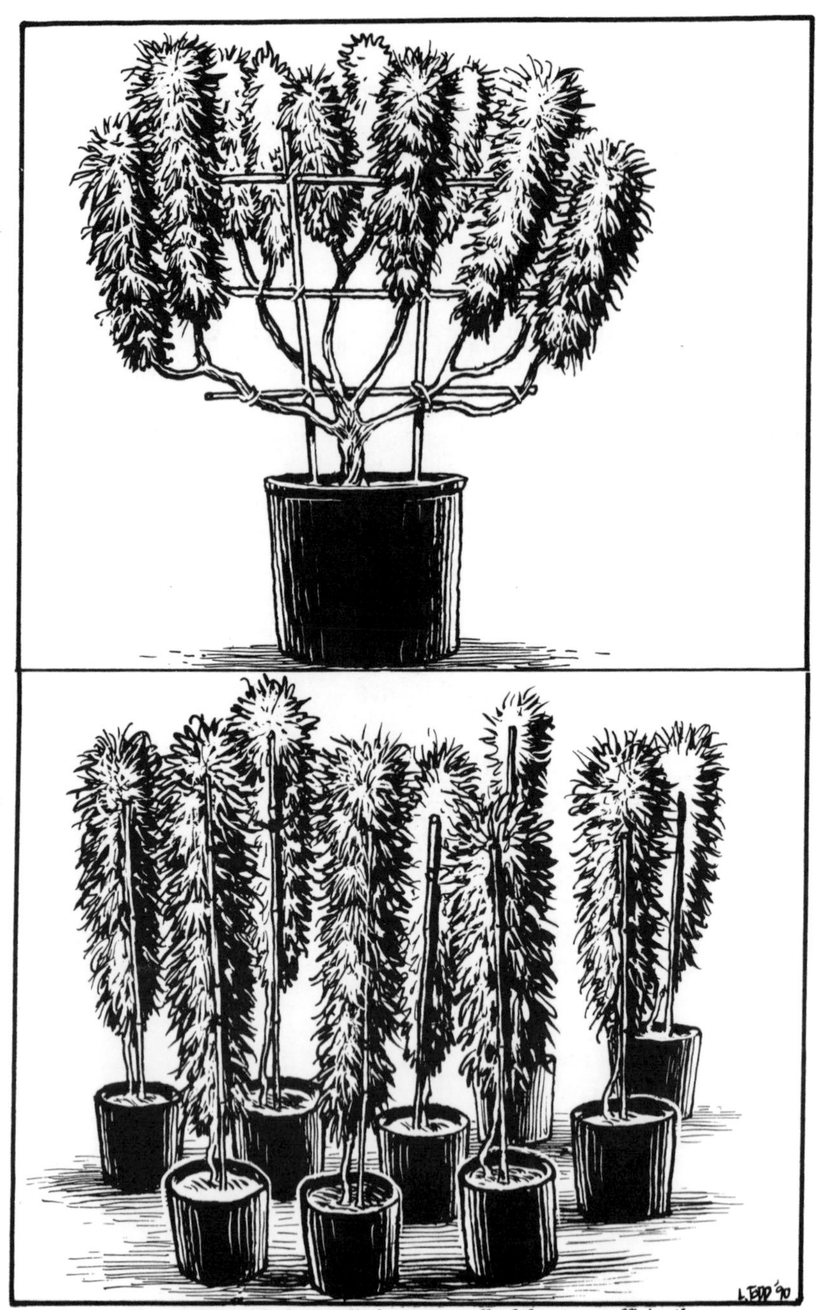

The garden with the small plants uses all of the space efficiently.

Chapter 2
PERSPECTIVE

Setting up and maintaining a successful indoor garden requires a bit of work and some hands-on experience. No one gets the garden running at full potential the first time out. Any farmer will say: "Don't count your chickens before they're hatched." Rather than setting up a gigantic sophisticated garden with little experience, the best growers start off with a less ambitious project which has more chance of success.

Small gardens are easier to maintain than large ones. They take less time, but more importantly, they do not have the problems of energy consumption, ventilation and heat that large gardens have. With a small system, the energy consumption does not go up that much. A large system using several large wattage lamps spins the meter. The heat created in a small system is easily dissipated into the surrounding environment, especially during cool months. A large system requires a more sophisticated heat-exchange system.

Marijuana has two distinct parts to its growing cycle. First it grows vegetatively, then it goes into flowering. During the vegetative cycle the plants receive lighting continuously or for a minimum of 18 hours a day. During the flowering cycle they receive fewer hours of light. For this reason it is convenient to separate any garden into two separate units, one for vegetative growth and one for flowering. The vegetative growth unit need not necessarily be large since it is used mostly for starting seeds and clones.

In the most efficient growing system, plants are grown in the vegetative section until they are 8-12 inches high and then are placed in the flowering area. The vegetative section requires about ⅓ the space of the flowering section.

Chapter 3
THE SPACE

Gardeners who I have observed have converted all kinds of spaces to grow rooms: closets, small rooms, pantries, basements, attics, and small sheds. The space must be high enough to allow the plants to grow to 2-3 feet height. A space 4 feet high can be converted into a garden. A space eight feet high can be converted into a two-level garden.

The area that a space covers is figured by multiplying the length by width. The result is the number of square feet. The size and number of lights used is based on the total area. When the garden is configured, aisle space is left between the plants, so that they can be attended easily. People have an effective reach of 2 to 3 feet, averaging around 2½. Usually aisles are 1½-2 feet wide. When the growing unit placed on moveable platforms, most aisle spaces can be eliminated. Aisles are made by simply moving the units.

Light fixtures and reflectors should hang from chains mounted directly to a stud, or using a molly bolt, into the lathing. A lamp's height is adjusted by changing its position on the chain. It is extremely important for the light to be hung securely. Should the reflector fall, it could cause an electrical short in a wet area, which is very dangerous, even life threatening.

Gardens are equipped with circuit interrupters, which functions as a circuit breaker. This unit shuts off the power in case of a short or an interruption in service.

THE FLOORS

The floors of the grow rooms I have seen have been well prepared. Smart growers protect the floors, especially wood or linoleum tile, from water using heavy plastic lining. If the grow room is in a basement or a cool room, where the temperature of the floor is always cool, either the surface has been insulated or the plants had been raised off the floor. This is very important because cold floors draw heat from the containers. Plants germinate and grow considerably slower when their roots are cold.

There are a number of ways growers insulate the floor. Styrofoam insulation, which comes in sheets or rolls, has been placed over the floors. This material has the added advantage that it is very reflective, so that any light hitting this surface bounces back to the plants. Plywood is often placed over a layer of insulating material. Plants are raised off a floor using a table or wooden boards. Shipping pallets provide air spaces so the warm air circulating in the room can reach the containers.

Heating the Roots

Cold roots slow growth to a crawl. Heating cables or a heating mat made for heating soil or containers keep the roots warm. Some cables and mats have a built-in thermostat to keep the temperature a constant 70-75 degrees. Heating cables and mats are available from many garden shops. They are convenient to use and consume only a few watts.

Growers use room temperature or lukewarm water to irrigate the plants so that the roots are not shocked and cooled down. They use lukewarm tap water, or heat the water in the reservoir. Small reservoirs (up to 100 gallons) are warmed using an aquarium heater and thermostat. Larger tanks are heated using a water heater. An ideal water temperature is 70 degrees.

Here are some floor plans from typical gardens.

1. A closet 9 feet high by 36 inches deep by 40 inches wide. This space did not have convenient dimensions for using fluorescents, so it was easiest to use a MH or HPS lamp (see page 28). The total space was about 10 square feet. A 250 watt MH lamp lit the space. A shelf was constructed at half the height. The shelf supported a second garden. Each garden was powered by a 250 watt MH lamp. Ventilation is provided by keeping the door open. No CO_2. See illustration on page 9.

2. A closet 8 feet high x 2 feet x 9 feet. As a single level unit the closet was originally illuminated by 4 8 ft. fluorescents. This was converted to a 400 watt MH mounted on a Solar Shuttle type track. The garden was modified to 2 shelf gardens. The top one still under the Solar Shuttle and MH. The bottom one uses two 250 watt HPS lamps permanently mounted. A small oscillating fan mounted on the top of each garden keeps the air flowing. Most of the time the doors are kept open. When they are closed, wide cracks between the doors help bring in fresh air. No CO_2. See illustration on page 10.

3. A room 9 feet high x 12 feet x 10 feet, all growing on one level. It is lit using a MH and a HPS, each 1000 watts. The lights rotate on a Whirlagig so that light is spread more evenly. Ventilation through a window fan regulated by a thermostat. CO_2 using a tank and regulator. Steel shelving with three levels, each 4′ x 2′ with 4 fluorescent tubes is light sealed from the rest of the room using opaque curtains. Clones are generated in this space.

   The room had 3 aisles. The first started along the door on the side of the room and extended most of the 12 foot length of the room. It was 24 inches wide. Two additional aisles branched off from the main aisle. They paralleled the width of the room and started at 2½ feet from the side wall. Each was 18″ wide. They each extended a length of 7 feet from the wall leaving a 2 foot growing space at the end of the garden. The total growing area of the garden was about 100 square feet including growing shelves.

   This room could have been configured as a shelf growing space using the same aisle space. Lighting would be provided by 400 watt HPS units mounted on the ceiling of each shelf. A total of 6 units would be used. Total growing area would be about 190 sq. ft.

   Ventilation from this space was via a fireplace. A one foot diameter tube sucked air from the top of the room and using a powerful fan mounted inside the tube, drove the air out. See illustration on page 11.

4. A basement space 5 x 5 feet 40 inches high. To conserve vertical space fluorescents were used. Ten were mounted permanently to the rafters overhanging the garden. Two 4 foot fluorescent tubes were mounted on each of three sides of the garden to encourage healthier growth. Reflective surface and heat preservation were accomplished by hanging mylar by the rafters along the perimeter of the garden. The floor is always cold so a thin piece of plywood was placed over a vinyl plastic sheet covering R11 insulation. A tank with regulator distributes CO_2. During winter, rather than trying to heat the air in the space, heating cables keep the roots and other plant surfaces warm. See illustration on page 12.

5. An attic garden. Raw attic space has been cordoned off by hanging reflective curtains of astrolon in an area 6 x 6 feet. A 400 watt HPS light is hung from the rafters over the garden. Draft provides ventilation. Growers have reported that attic gardens have a lot of problems because they are subject to severe weather shifts and extreme seasonal

conditions. If an area can be contained, either by building walls or using heavy curtains, it is easier to maintain reasonable growing temperatures. In winter, temperatures can be raised using a gas heater regulated for indoor use. The heater emits CO_2 as well as heat. During the summer attics must sometimes be abandoned because the temperature gets too high. See illustration on page 13.

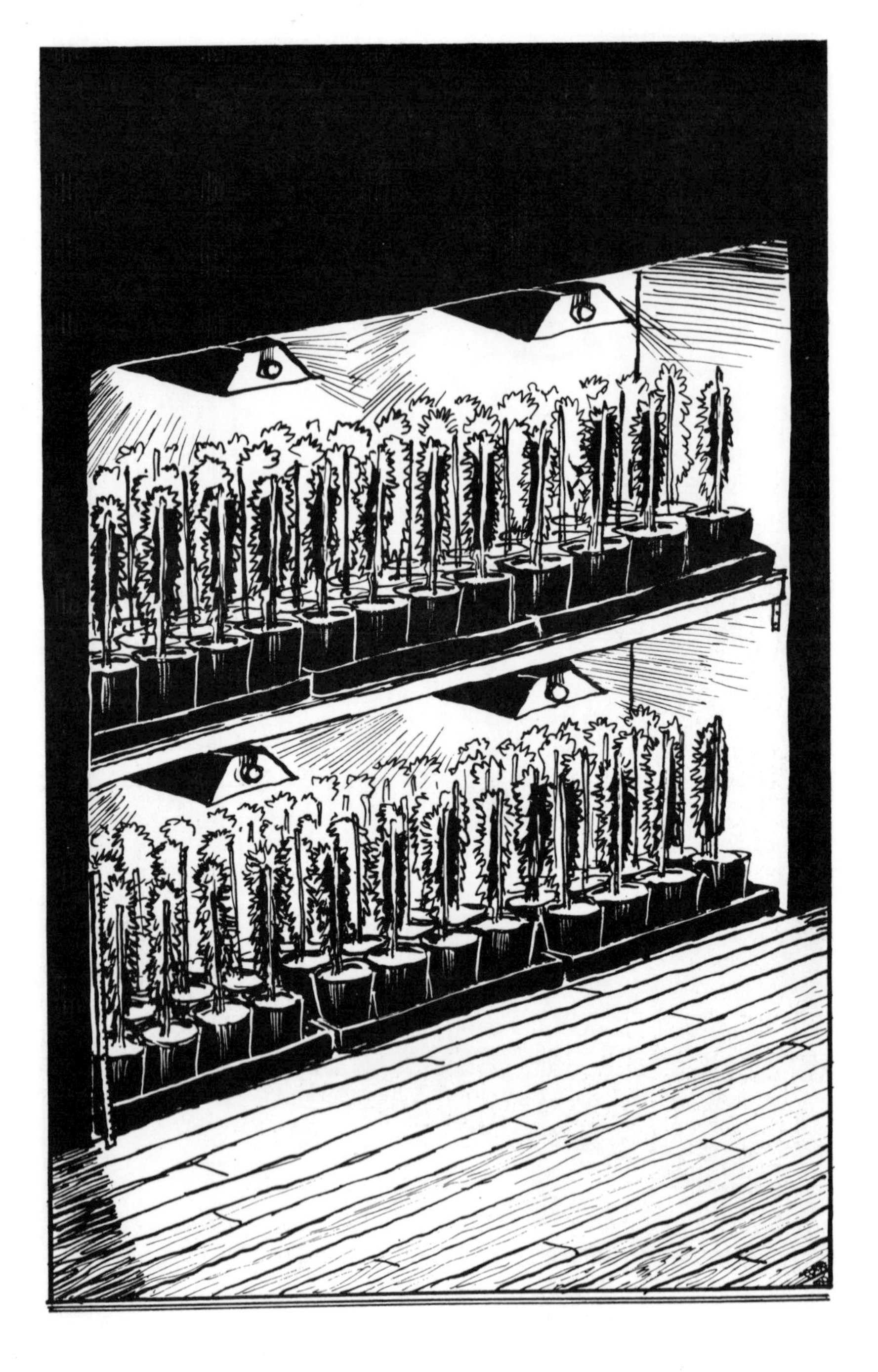

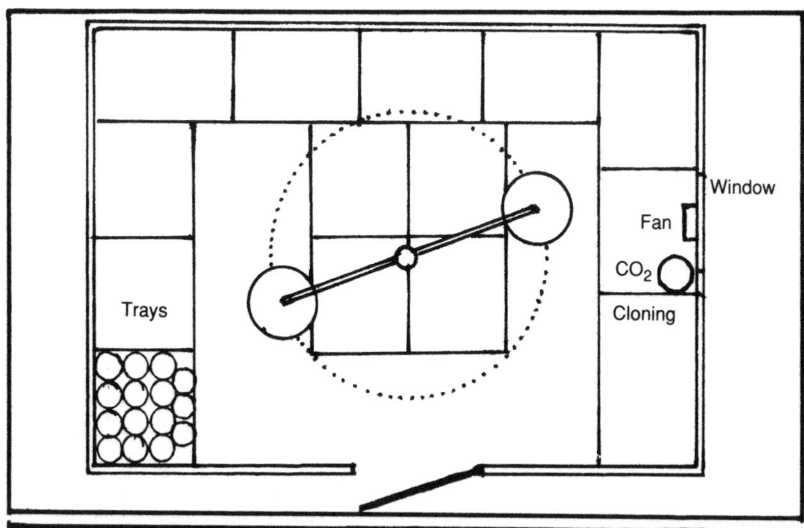
Window
Fan
CO_2
Trays
Cloning

CO_2

Chapter 4
NOVEL GARDENS

Marijuana, which would grow so easily on a windowsill or in a garden, must be hidden from unfriendly eyes. Still, people want to try their hand growing this plant. Human ingenuity is a wonderful thing. So is cannabis' ability to adapt to unusual growing conditions. Here are some novel ways that marijuana has been grown.

1. Training to a fence. Marijuana can be controlled so that it does not have much of a 3 dimensional shape by tying the branches to a fence. Here is a typical example. A gardener had a space which was 30" x 15" and 9 feet high between two shelves in a storage area. The walls were covered with aluminum foil. Chicken wire with two inch holes was stretched to a frame of 1" x 2"'s on one of the lengthwise wall. Six 8 foot fluorescents were placed vertically on the other side of the garden so that the light was coming to the plants from the side. Three shelves were built to hold two foot long window boxes.

   As the plants grew, their stems were gently spread and tied to the fence with metal twist-ties. The third dimension was almost entirely eliminated. Since the plants configuration was well controlled, the gardener controlled the spacing and helped light to reach all plant parts.

2. Some growers build training stakes for their plants. These are actually wooden stakes with cross stakes attached. Growers tie the plants to the guides as they grow. The stakes are configured for maximum exposure to the light. Excess growth is trimmed so that the plant conforms to the pattern set by the stakes. See illustration on page 17.

3. Horizontalizing. Marijuana uses gravity to sense which direction is "up" and then grows that way. When a plant which has been growing normally is placed on its side, new growth reorients itself and starts growing up. Growers with short spaces can sometimes maximize the space in their garden by taking a plant and placing it horizontally. See illustration on page 18.

4. Selective Pruning. Marijuana grows branches in four directions, first in opposite pairs and then alternating. By pruning two opposite sides of the plant, it grows flat naturally. The branches can be tied down a bit so that branches of two plants can be alternated. See illustration on page 19.

5. A space was only 2½ feet high, 13″ wide and 5 ft. long. A four tube flat fluorescent unit, designed for ceiling installation, was placed against one wall. The other wall was lined with a single row of 6 inch containers. See illustration on page 20.

L. TODD.'90

Chapter 5
THE PLANT

Years ago people grew seeds from their best stash, mostly sativas, originating in Colombia and Mexico. These plants grow in a classic conical shape, with long spreading limbs at the bottom and a single main stem on the top. Since then, Americans have discovered many other varieties such as single-stem Moroccans, asymetrical indicas, and variants such as "creepers." There are thousands of varieties of marijuana. They have different potential yields, highs, flower size, bud structure, ripening time, height, leaf shape, color, bushiness, and amount of light required for adequate growth

In much the same way that the environment affects the yield and flavor of grapes, it also affects the genetic potential of marijuana. The taste, quality of the high, yield, and color are all subject to modification by the environment. Some of the factors include amount and quality of light, water, temperature, amount, ratios and kinds of fertilizers or nutrients, and cultivation practices.

The Marijuana Lifecycle

Marijuana is an annual plant. Each spring the plants germinate and begin a period of rapid growth. As fall approaches, the plants' growth changes from vegetative to flowering or reproductive. Female and male flowers are found on separate plants. To produce seeds, pollen from male plants must fertilize the female flowers. When the male plants are removed from the garden, the females remain unfertilized. The resulting clusters of virgin flowers are called sinsemilla, which means "without seeds" in Spanish. These "buds" are prized by the marijuana connoisseur.

Undisturbed by gardeners, the male plants release their pollen into the air, lose vigor, and die. The female plants continue to produce flowers for quite a while as long as they remain unfertilized. Once fertilized, the small ovary found behind each flower begins to swell, and within a few weeks, mature seeds are produced. When most of the flowers are fertilized, the plant ceases to produce new flowers. Instead, most of its energy goes to the maturing seeds. As the seeds mature, the plant loses vigor and dies.

The Modern Plant

In the past few years the breeders at the Dutch seed companies have popularized new strains especially bred for indoor growing. Many varieties are available which are high yielding, potent and compact. For most gardeners, Dutch seeds are their best choice. While the price of these commercial seeds may seem costly at first, getting the best seed stock is the most inexpensive way to improve a garden. No matter how good the system or attentive the care of the plants, if they do not have the potential for massive high quality buds, they will never produce them. A seed does not represent just a single plant, but an entire genetic line. New plants are cloned by growers from plants or more seeds can be produced which carry this heritage.

Marijuana varieties are often categorized as either sativa or indica. Indica plants tend to grow compact with heavy dense buds, relatively short stature and a minimum of wide branching. Sativas used to be gangly, with smaller buds. Now they have been bred to grow smaller with heavier yields. When marijuana plants are forced early the new sativas and indica plants gain 25-100 percent height. However the older sativa varieties, even when forced at a short height may continue to grow into a large size plant. This makes them unacceptable for growing in short height gardens.

Chapter 6
VARIETIES

Growers have been breeding and adapting marijuana to indoor growing since the late 60's. Starting with equatorial and indica strains, breeders have produced faster growing, more potent varieties. Although this work has been done informally, the net effect of having thousands of breeders working has been the equivalent of a national program to improve quality.

Since the opening of the marijuana seed companies in Holland, growers in the United States have easy access to many excellent varieties. Some of the varieties well adapted to closet cultivation are listed below.

SKUNK #1- Developed by Sacred Seeds and produced by both Seed Bank (SB) and S.S.S.C.. It is a stabilized indica-sativa hybrid with a strong odor and very potent, pleasant high. It is fairly high yielding and can be grown with high intensity lights indoors. It has a moderate internode (length between leaves) length. Excellent for greenhouses or skylights. For indoor growers Skunk is used for hybridizing.

NORTHERN LIGHTS- An indica hybrid bred by northwest growers and popularized by the Seed Bank. This variety does very well in grow rooms because of relatively low light requirements. It is a compact and is easily kept short. Northern Lights buds are among the most potent in the world. It has quite a distinctive "personality." It is often hybridized with distinctive plants.

EARLY PEARL- An indica-sativa hybrid developed at a midwestern university. It has a nice, up high, pleasant taste and is strong. Very fast maturing but it has fairly long internodes.

BIG BUD- A variety with a dense smoke, and indica high. It is very high yielding, with a large bud on a compact plant. However it is very finicky, needs a lot of light and is difficult to clone. It has been phased out of the Seed Bank's catalog but is still being used by cultivators.

All of these varieties have been stabilized a bit. They are often hybridized with each other.

Chapter 7
PLANT REQUIREMENTS

A plant's growth rate, high and yield determined mostly by its genetic material. No matter how well the plant's needs are met, it can only grow up to its potential.

The environmental factors affecting plant growth are light, root conditions, water, nutrients, temperature and air (CO_2 and O_2). A plant can grow only as fast as the weakest link on the chain permits. For instance, when a plant which receives all of the light, water, and CO_2 it can use, without adequate nutrients, its growth is thwarted.

"Growth is limited by the least available requirement"

Chapter 8
LIGHT

Plants use light as energy to fuel photosynthesis, a process in which water and carbon dioxide (CO_2) are the raw materials used to make sugar. Sugar is the basic building block of all plants. By twisting the sugar molecule, plants form carbohydrates, which are more complex molecules. Plants use carbohydrates to build tissue. When nitrogen atoms are integrated into the molecules, amino acids are formed. These are eventually grouped together to form proteins.

Light is also used to regulate many varieties of cannabis' reproductive cycle. Scientists speculate that the plant produces a hormone during the dark period (night in nature) which induces the start of the reproductive (flowering) cycle. When the hormone builds up to a critical level, flower growth commences. The number of hours of darkness required to induce flowering differs for each variety.

Gardeners have a choice of lamps to illuminate their garden. Incandescents, tungsten-halogen lamps and screw in "grow bulbs" are inefficient sources of light. Although they are inexpensive to purchase, their cost of operation makes them the costliest source of light.

FLUORESCENTS

Until the early 1980's most indoor growers used fluorescent lights to illuminate the garden. These tubes have tremendous advantages over screw-in incandescent lights. A fluorescent tube emits about 3 times as much light as an incandescent of the same wattage and has a light spectrum that plants can use more efficiently.

Fluorescents have their limitations. Light is emitted over a large area, the entire surface of the tube, so it is not concentrated. Because the tubes are bulky, only a limited amount of light can be delivered to a given area. The fixtures are usually placed within inches of the plants so that the light does not spread and become less intense. When the light fixtures are hung, they are hard to manipulate and make it more difficult to tend the garden.

Standard fluorescents have an efficiency of about 30%. Seventy percent of the electricity is not turned into light but into heat. There are newer types which are a little more efficent, but the increase in light is of only marginal help.

VHO (very high output) FLUORESCENTS are also available. They use about 3 times the electricity of standard fluorescents and emit about 2½ times the light. While they are not as efficient as regular fluorescents, each tube delivers 2½ times more light to the garden.

The inner surface of each fluorescent tube is covered with a phosphor which glows when tickled by the flow of electrons through it. Fluorescent tubes are named for the spectrum of light which they emit. Some of the spectrums are more conducive to plant growth than others. Deluxe warm white, warm white, and deluxe cool white are three types which promote fast growth. Special grow bulbs concentrate light in areas used most efficiently by the plant. However, they are fairly dim and plant growth is slowed when they are used.

HIGH INTENSITY DISCHARGE LAMPS

High intensity discharge lamps (HIDs) are easier to use and more efficient. Low wattage HIDs are sometimes sold for household outdoor use. Large wattage lamps are used to light yards, streets, parking lots, stadiums and other large areas. They come in two versions:

METAL HALIDES or MH lamps emit a white light that looks slightly bluish. They are used to light stadiums, convention centers and other large areas where a natural looking light is desired.

HIGH PRESSURE SODIUM or HPS lamps emit a pink or amber light. They are used to illuminate parking lots and other areas where the color of the light is not important. HPS units are more efficient than MH lamps. They are often used alone with no detrimental effect to the plants, and will promote faster plant growth than MH bulbs during both vegetative growth and flowering. Combinations of bulbs are not required, as the HPS lamp has all the light spectrums necessary for healthy growth.

MH lamps come in 175, 250, 400 and 1000 watt sizes. HPS lamps come in 150, 400 and 1000 watt sizes. Each lamp has its own ballast.

HID lighting systems are much more convenient to use than fluorescents because the lamps have a higher wattage and are more efficient at producing light than fluorescents. Large wattage systems are more efficient than smaller ones. MH lamps have an efficiency of 35-50%

depending on the wattage. HPS lamps have an efficiency of 50-55%. Moving the lamp and reflector is fairly easy since they are fairly light. The light is powered by a heavy ballast, but it is connected only by a long electrical wire. Some 400 watt HID systems are manufactured with the ballast built into the same housing as the reflector. These lamps are harder to move around and are usually considered for lighting only if they are to be permanently mounted.

This chart shows how much light each lamp emits, its lumen output per 100 watts and the area it covers adequately.

Watts	# Of Lumens Emitted	# Of Lumens Per 100 Watts	Square Feet Illuminated
100 W Incandescent	1,750	1,750	N/Applicable
4′ Fl. (CW-40W)	2,960	7,400	1-2
8′ Fl. (CW-75W)	5,800	7,733	2-4
MH 175W	14,000	8,000	5-10
MH 400W	40,000	10,000	12-20
MH 1000W	125,000	12,500	35-70
HPS 100W	9,500	9,500	3-6
HPS 150W	16,000	10,600	5-10
HPS 400W	50,000	125,000	15-30
HPS 1000	140,000	14,000	40-80

Because of the ease and convenience of operating a HID lamp and their increased efficiency they are recommended for lighting indoor gardens.

Gardens should receive between 1000-3000 lumens per square foot. Of course, plants in a 3000 lumen garden will grow faster and flower more profusely than those under dimmer lights. Successful gardens usually are lit at between 1500-2500 lumens per square foot. During the vegetative stage, plants stretch out when they receive low levels of light. During flowering, the flowers are looser and sparse.

This chart shows the approximate amount of light received by gardens of various sizes with a very efficient reflector. Twenty percent of the light emitted has been deducted from the total to correct for reflector inefficiency and light which never reaches the garden. Light is never distributed evenly so some parts of the garden will get more light than others.

Garden Size	# of Sq. Feet	# of Lumens Per Square Foot MH 400	MH 1000	HPS 400	HPS 1000
3′ x 3′	9	3,500	11,100	4,450	12,450.
4′ x 4′	16	2,000	6,250	2,500	7,000
5′ x 5′	25	1,300	4,000	2,000	4,500
6′ x 6′	36	900	2,800	900	3,100
7′ x 7′	49	650	2,050	650	2,300
8′ x 8′	64	500	1,560	390	1,750
9′ x 9′	81	400	1,250	500	1,400
10′ x 10′	100	300	1,000	400	1,100

LIGHTS AND REFLECTORS

Sunlight comes from a distant source, so that the light rays hitting a small portion of planet Earth (say a garden 12 feet wide) are virtually parallel. Their intensity does not diminish over the length of a plant 6 feet tall.

Light emitted from tubes and lamps travels in all directions. As the distance from the lamp increases, the intensity of the light decreases. It is not that any light is lost, just that the same amount of light is spread over larger area.

HID lamps and reflectors come in two configurations. Either the lamps are held vertically or horizontally:

Horizontally held lamps direct most of the light downward because the light is emitted along the length of the lamp. Only a small reflector is required to beam the rest of the light downward.

Vertical lights emit most of their light horizontally. In order to reach a garden, the light must be reflected downward using a large, bulky reflector. Manufacturers have developed elaborate and innovative hoods, still they cannot reach the light delivery efficiency of a horizontal lamp.

Horizontally held lamps have several other advantages over verticals. They take less vertical space, which is crucial for short gardens, and the reflectors are much less bulky. All in all, horizontally held lamps are considered the best configuration for the closet garden.

Aluminum reflectors deliver the most light, more than white ones. Stainless steel reflectors absorb some spectrums of light and should not be used. See illustration on page 31.

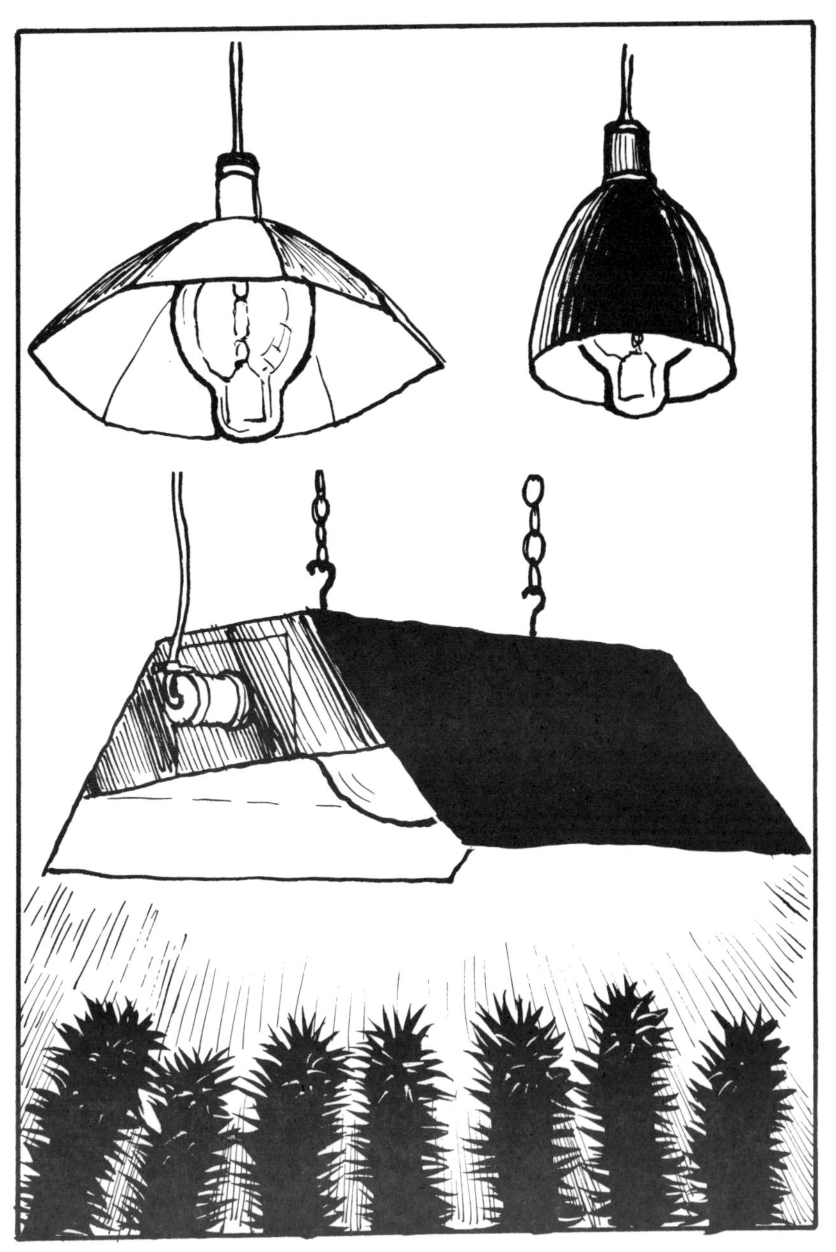

A small horizontal reflector actually delivers more light to the garden below than this large horizontal reflector. The small vertical reflector allows much of the light to escape to the sides.

FLUORESCENT LIGHT REFLECTORS

A garden lit by two tubes per foot of width with a high quality reflector receives about 1,100 lumens per square foot. A garden lit by three tubes per foot of width receives about 1700 lumens per square foot.

Fluorescents come in many lengths, but the two most commonly used by indoor gardeners are 4 and 8 ft. lengths. They are convenient to use and are more efficient than other sizes.

Poorly designed fluorescent fixtures, with no baffles between the tubes to reflect light downward may lose up to 40% of the light. Instead, tubes are mounted onto a reflector with individual baffles between the tubes so that light is directed downward to the garden. A good reflector may keep losses down to 20%. An alternative is to use tubes with reflective surfaces. These are made several manufacturers. Often stores do not carry them but will special order them. See illustration on page 33.

New fluorescent configurations have made it easier to build a garden. Circle tubes and thin tubed 8" doubles screw into incandescent sockets. Although these bulbs are not very efficient they are step up from incandescents. Combinations of circle lights and tubes can illuminate a garden very brightly. They can be used in extremely small spaces. These lamps always seem to be on sale. When electrical costs are not a factor they are a inexpensive way of setting up a garden. See illustration on page 34.

As tubes age they become less efficient. On the average, they lose 25% of light they were rated for after about a year of use. Lights which are turned on and off a lot wear out faster. Three to six inch sections on both sides of the tube dull out from deposits after a short term of use. Growers figure the effective length of a 4 ft tube as 3 feet 4 inches and of an 8 ft tube as 7 feet.

Light Spectrums and Photosynthesis

Each source of light has a characteristic spectrum, which is caused by the varying wave lengths of light therein. Fluorescents and other electric lights emit different shades of light. To our eyes mid-day summer sunlight looks neutral, incandescent lights have a reddish tint, fluorescents vary in spectrum according to their type, MH lamps a have a blue coolness to them and HPS lamps look pink-amber.

To produce chlorophyll, plants need light from specific spectrums, (TABLE 1, page 35) mainly red and blue. This is called the chloroplast light spectrum. Once the chlorophyll is produced, a slightly different spectrum

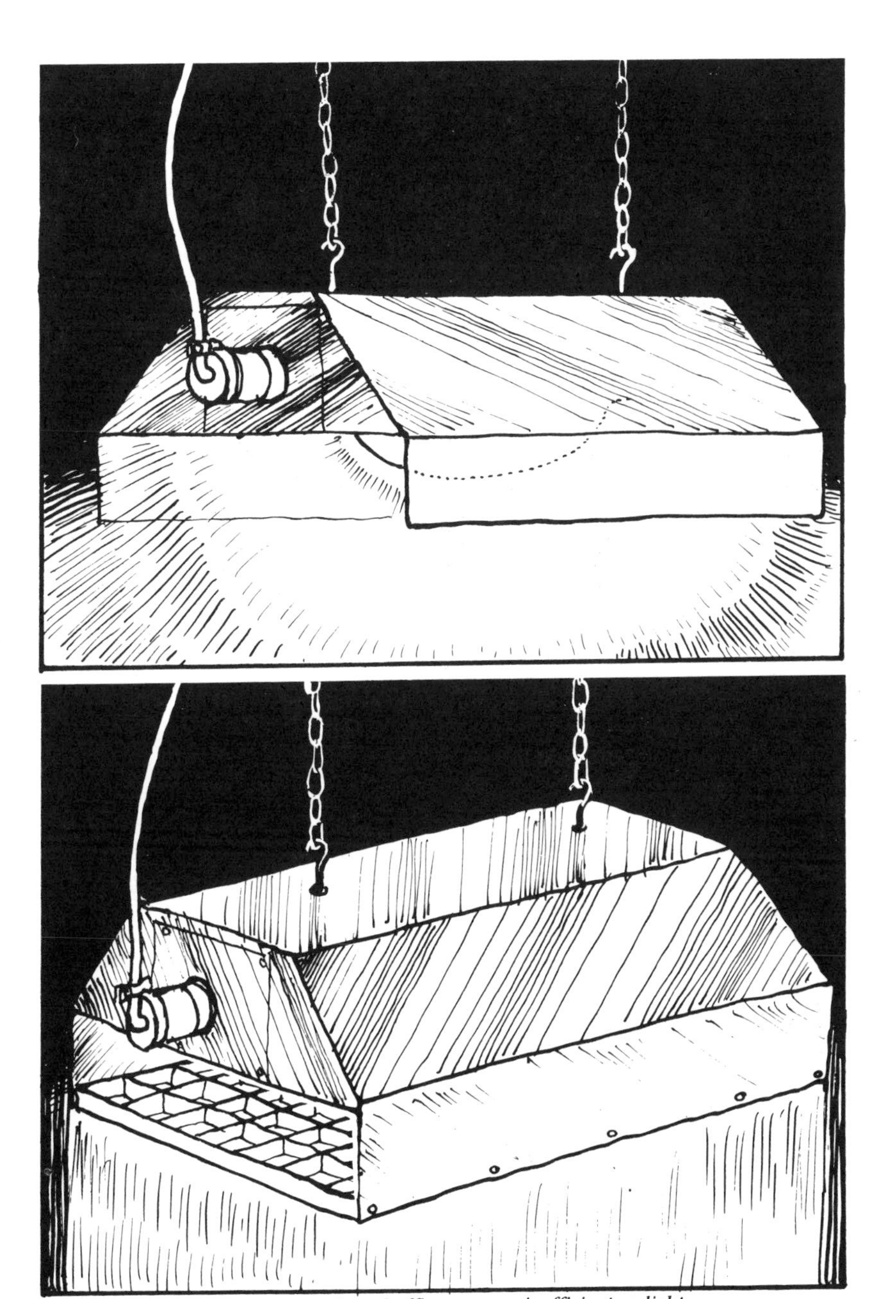

Reflectors without baffles are very inefficient so light is lost. Baffles direct the light downward.

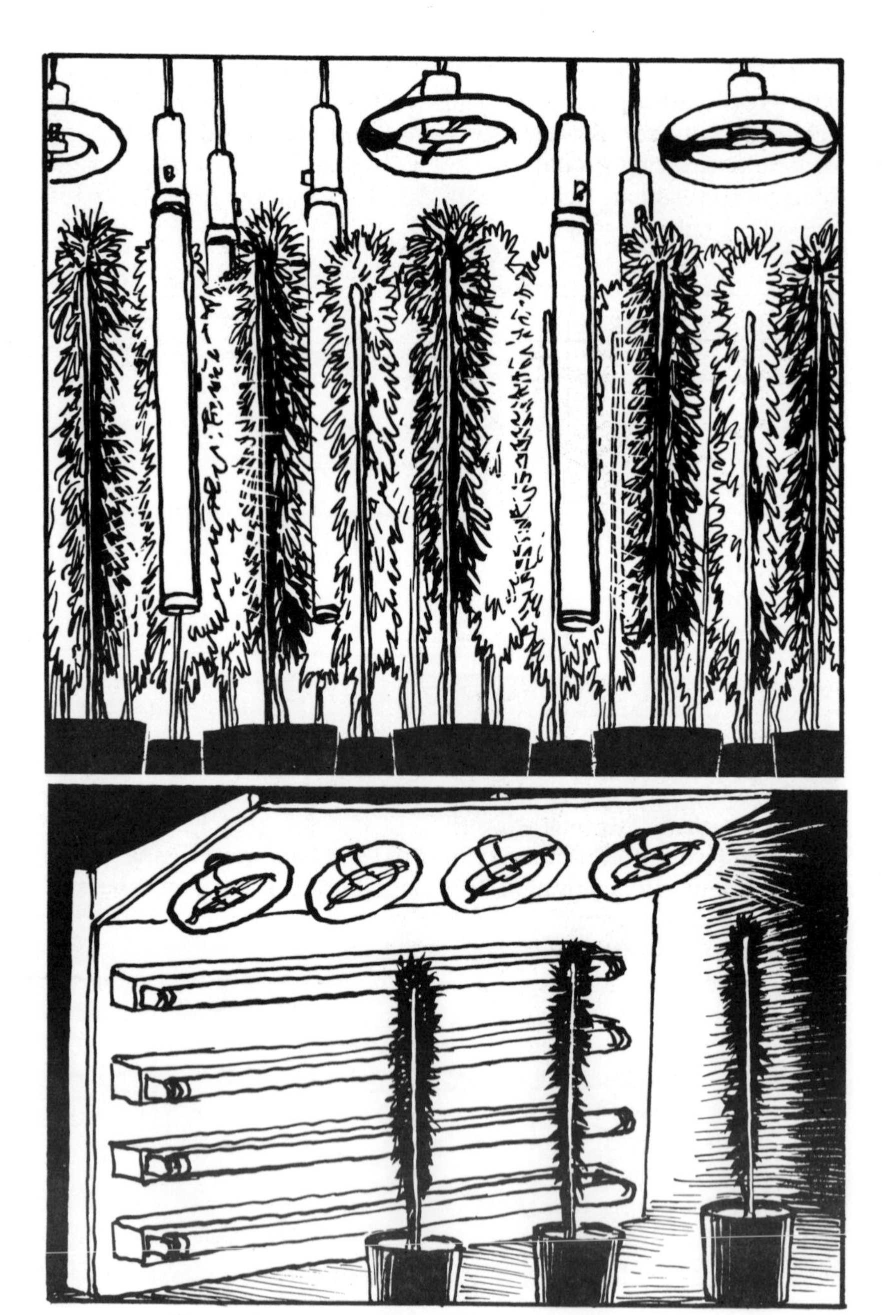

These units easily provide over 2000 lumens per square foot.

of light (TABLE 1) is used by the plant for photosynthesis, the process which results in the production of sugars. Plants use red and blue light most efficiently but they also use use orange and yellow light. Plants are continually growing, producing new chloroplasts and chlorophyll so both spectrums of light are being used by the plant continually. Plants reflect green light rather than using it.

TABLE 1 - Action Spectrum of: (A) Photosynthetic Response, and (B) Chlorophyll Synthesis

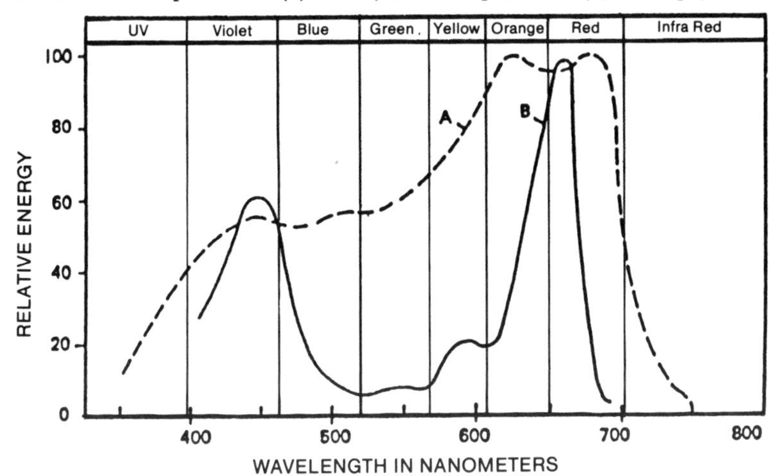

Although the MH and HPS lamps emit different color light both lamps emit high levels of light in the critical red and blue wavelengths. Either lamp can be used for cultivation. HPS lamps produce faster growth because they emit more total light useable by the plant.

Many shop owners maintain that combinations of MH and HPS lights produce the fastest growth, or alternatively, that MH units should be used for growth and HPS units for flowering. There is no indication that either of these theories holds up. HPS lamps produce faster growth than a combination of HPS and MH lamps. There is absolutely no need to or advantage to buying a MH unit. Plants grown under HPS show some stem etoliation (stretching) and ripen about a week later. This is more than compensated with a considerably larger crop.

Some fluorescent tube manufacturers produce grow tubes which are especially formulated to provide a spectrum of light similar to the chlorophyll synthesis or photosynthesis spectrum or a compromise between them. The idea is sound, but grow tubes produce only 35-60% of the light of a cool white fluorescent, and less light useable by the plant. One manufacturer advertises Vita-Lite® and Optima® fluorescent tubes which emit a light spectrum color balanced close to the sun's spectrum. However, they emit only 75% of the light of a warm white fluorescent.

COSTS

HPS systems are the most expensive to purchase of all of the lighting units. MH units are a little cheaper and fluorescents are the cheapest of all. However, this is figuring only the intial outlay. Factoring in the cost per unit of light produced, the positions are reversed. HPS lamps are the cheapest, followed by MH lamps and far behind come the fluorescents. In addition HID lamps are considered easier to work with in the garden and produce a better crop than fluorescents.

Cost in cents per 1000 lumens of various lamps. (Expressed in cents per kilowatt)

		Cost Per Kilowatt Hour Of Electricity			
Lamp	Output	8¢	10¢	12¢	16¢
100W Incandescent	1,750	.46	.57	.68	.91
4' Fl. (CW-40W)	2,960	.11	.13	.16	.22
175W MH	14,000	.10	.12	.15	.20
400W MH	40,000	.08	.10	.12	.16
1000W MH	125,000	.06	.08	.10	.13
100W HPS	9,500	.08	.10	.13	.17
400W HPS	50,000	.06	.08	.10	.13
1000HPS	140,000	.06	.07	.08	.11

Note about the chart: These figures denote the part of a cent used to produce 1000 lumens. In dollar terms the figures for a 1000 HPS are \$.0006, \$.0007, \$.0008, \$.0011.

Step By Step

1. The successful gardens I have observed use a minimum of 1000 lumens per sq. ft. during vegetative growth and 1500 lumens during flowering. These figures are bare minimums, the more light the better. Gardens with 1500-2500 lumens during vegetative growth and 2000-3500 during flowering seem to do best.

2. The most efficient light source is a HPS lamp in a horizontal reflector. No other light source is needed. An HPS lamp supplies all the spectrums of light needed by the plant for normal growth.

Chapter 9
LIGHTING ACCESSORIES

Both fluorescent fixtures and HID lamps use a much higher voltage of electricity than standard 110 volt house current. Fluorescent fixtures contain a ballast or transformer that converts electricity to its proper voltage. HID lamps sometimes come in a fixture containing the ballast, but most of the units made for indoor gardens are designed with the ballast remote (separate, but connected by an electrical cord) from the lamp and reflector.

HID's with remote ballasts are much more convenient than units with the ballasts enclosed since they weigh less. 400 watt ballasts weigh about 28 lbs. and 1000 watt ballasts weigh about 40 lbs. It is much harder to manipulate and secure a heavy object like that overhead than it is to just leave it near ground level attached to the lamp by an electrical cord. The lamp is hung from the ceiling using cord or wire attached to a hook or pulley.

Light Movers

Outdoors, plants receive light from many directions. Over the course of the day the sun bathes plants in light starting in the east and travelling west. Leaves shaded during part of the day are under full sun at other times.

Indoors, using a stationary light, some plant parts are always shaded while others are always lit. With a light in the center of the garden, plants closer to the source receive brighter light than those at the periphery.

Reflectors with different shapes distribute light in varying patterns. A good quality reflector will spread the light evenly over the garden. Still, a light coming from a single stationary source leaves some areas in permanent shadow.

Light movers were invented to solve these problems. The movers carry the lamp over a fixed course so that entire the garden comes directly under the light part of the time. These units are manufactured by a number of suppliers and use several innovative techniques to move the lamps. Some of them move the lamps quickly, so that the light passes over the garden in less than a minute. Other movers take 40 minutes to traverse the course. Both types improve light distribution in the garden. As a result, the plants grow at an even rate. Since the plants are not stretching in one direction to the light, they grow straighter, with more symetry.

The rotating units seem most effective in a square room, while the shuttles, which go back and forth, seem best in rectangular or odd shaped spaces. See illustration on page 41.

REFLECTIVE MATERIAL

Closet cultivators have found that electrically generated light is precious so any generated is best conserved. Efficient indoor gardens must reflect back the light straying out of the perimeter. Growers cover walls which cannot be painted with flat white paint, with aluminum foil, Astrolon or mylar. This is extremely important. Any light which hits a dark surface is absorbed and converted into heat, rather than being used in the garden. Reflective material is easily hung using staples tacks or tape. There are several ways growers make walls very reflective:

White reflective paint. Flat white paint defracts the light so that it is distributed more evenly through the garden. Off-whites absorb a considerable amount of light so they are avoided. The best paint for indoor gardens is greenhouse white which is formulated for maximum reflectivity.

Aluminum foil is used to line the walls. It is highly reflective and very inexpensive. Its downsides are that is noisy when it moves with a breeze and has little tensile strength, so that it tears easily when not attached to a surface. It is usually not used where it will be moved around or used for a curtain or doorway because it crinkles and tears easily. When the dull side out is used the reflection is defused rather than just reflecting hot spots. Eighteen inch wide heavy duty rolls are the easiest to work with. In places where heat must be conserved fiberglass insulation with aluminum reflective surface is often used to line the walls.

Silvered gift wrap comes in rolls or sheets. It is composed of a thin metal foil glued onto paper wrap. It is very reflective, easy to use and inexpensive. It is available from some wholesale gift paper houses or from gift shops.

Styrofoam is used in cool spaces where heat must be conserved. The walls can be lined with styrofoam insulating material which comes on a roll or in sheets. (available in some home-improvement stores). It is extremely reflective. The rolls come in several widths, and is about 1/8″ thick.

Whirlagig & Solar Shuttle

Mylar. Grow stores sell silvered mylar which is extremely reflective. While mylar reflects most of the light, it is not opaque and it allows a dim image through. The plastic film creases easily.

Astrolon is a silvered plastic which is extremely reflective, but not opaque. The thin plastic is quilted and very pliable. It is very durable and very reflective.

Step by Step

1. Successful closet cultivators know that light should be distributed evenly throughout the grow space. Light movers or several lights may be indicated.

2. Smart growers line the walls of the growing area with a reflective surface to conserve light.

Chapter 10
ROOTS AND CONTAINERS

Roots serve plants in several ways. They hold the plant in position and they are its primary means of obtaining water and nutrients. The size and efficiency of the root system has a great effect upon the development of the plant and ultimately, upon its yield.

The amount of space that the roots have to grow depends on the cubic space of the container and the size of the particles in the growing medium. Roots growing around large sized particles obviously have less room than roots growing through small sized particles.

The size of the container is determined by the final size that the gardener intends for the plants. When plants are grown to the same size in different size containers the plant grown in the larger container is lusher, with more branching and more vigorous growth.

Usually gardeners use a container for each plant. This allows them maximum flexibility in moving the plants in the garden. However, using the techniques described in the book, trays holding a group of plants are just as convenient to use. Trays provide more room for the roots to spread out as well as more total cubic space than individual containers. Once a group of plants is established in a tray, the only way a plant can be removed is by clipping it off, or the other plants' roots may be disturbed.

Cannabis is very easy to transplant so plants are often moved to larger size containers as they grow.

Size of Containers

The chart on the next page shows the maximum size plants that containers can hold.

Most containers have less space than you would think because they are round and tapered.

Size of container	cubic in.	plant height	approx age
2 inch (2″x2″x2)	5	4-6 inches	10-15 days
3 inch (3″x3″x3″)	15		will allow the seedlings to spread out more during the initial growth period. It more than triples the cubic space.
4 inch (4″x4″x4″)	40	12″	20-35 days
5 inch (5″x5″x5″)	80	20″	some plants are no higher than 20″ at maturity
6″ (6″x6″x6″)	120	36″	indicas are rarely higher than this.
10″ (10″x10″x10″)	640	60″	sativas are rarely taller than this indoors

One way to increase the amount of material a container holds is to increase its height. An additional 1 inch depth to a 4 inch container increases its capacity by 16 cubic inches.

1 quart = 57.75 cubic inches

1 gallon = 231 cubic inches

Container sizes are notoriously inaccurate. Some "6 inch" containers are really five inches, and the standard "1 gallon" container is usually about 3 quarts.

Growers make sure all containers have large holes on the bottom or sides to allow for drainage.

A grower cannot go wrong growing a plant to maturity in a square six-inch container. The roots will have enough room to support healthy vigorous bud growth.

Step by Step

1. Plant roots need adequate space to grow. The more space the roots have, the larger the topside growth.

2. There are a number of choices regarding containers. Trays provide the most space but do not allow the convenience of being able to move individual plants. Most gardeners choose individual containers.

3. A Two inch square container supports a plant 4″-6.″ A 4 inch to 1 foot. A 5 inch to 2 feet. A 6 inch to 3 feet. Mature plants do very well in a 6″ container.
4. An easy way growers provide more space to the roots is by increasing container depth.

Chapter 11
THE PLANTING MEDIUM

The growing medium holds the roots firmly so that they can support the plant, and holds the water-nutrient solution and air so that they are available to the plants. It is obvious that the roots are used by the plant to obtain water and nutrients, but they need oxygen too. Roots not obtaining sufficient oxygen become sickly and are attacked by mildews and rots.

Planting mediums range the spectrum from totally organic to artificial materials. Organic materials such as compost, topsoil, humus, worm castings and steer manure have nutrients tied up in complex molecules.

Almost everyone has grown a houseplant. After the plant was in the container for a while, its growth slowed for 2 reasons: the roots were potbound and the nutrients in the planting medium were used up. When some fertilizer was added to the water, the plant showed renewed vigor.

The inert soil held the water-nutrient solution but did not supply nutrients of its own. The container became a simple hydroponic unit. The nutrients in the fertilizer were in soluble form and immediately available to the plant through the water.

Most books take a vehement stand on the advantages of hydroponics vs. soil for indoor cultivation. We are courageously sticking to a non-judgmental middle ground. Almost everyone growing marijuana indoors delivers at least part of the nutrients mixed in water. This is, of course, hydroponic.

Many growers make a nutrient rich "planting mix" or use top soil. These mediums support growth for some time without additional fertilization, but they are not "natural." Frankly, it is impossible to get a mini-eco-system going in each container or tray. It does not matter to the plant. As long as its needs are met, it thrives.

Some growers maintain that earth based systems produce tastier crops, but I have experienced some appetizing hydroponic product, and in fact the best tasting tomato I ever ate was grown in a hydroponic store's sunlit growing unit. Various books and magazines advise that hydroponic growing is more exacting and less forgiving than organic growing methods. In fact, hydroponic growing takes no more expertise or skill than growing in soil based mediums.

Here is a list of ingredients for planting mixes:

TOPSOIL - is a rich mixture of decaying organic matter and minerals which is the uppermost and richest layer of soil. It is sold in nurseries for use outdoors. It is looks dark brown, almost black and smells earthy. It is about as organic as you can get. However, it is not sterilized or pasteurized, so it may contain pests or pest eggs as well as fungi and diseases. This is usually not a problem though. Although topsoil works well in the ground, it is a heavy in containers and clumps or packs unless used with other ingredients which lighten it. Packed soil prevents water being distributed unevenly. Part of the medium becomes soaked, while the other part remains dry.

COMPOST - is an earthy smelling almost black, crumbly mixture containing decayed plant matter. It is teeming with life and although not necessarily high in nutrients, it provides a rich environment for the roots. It is acidic unless limed. Some commercial composts are nothing more than chopped up dried plant matter. This material may add some organic matter to the soil, but is not the same as real compost.

WORM CASTINGS - is compost digested by worms. As they digest the ingredients they concentrate them so that the nutrients are readily available to the plants. It is a excellent ingredient in mixes.

HUMUS - is a compost produced in a very moist environment. It is very fine textured and rich in nutrients, but quite acidic.

COMMERCIAL POTTING MIXES - are not soils at all, but mixes containing ingredients such as tree bark, peat moss, wood by-products, as well as artificial ingredients. These mixes have virtually no nutrient value unless fertilizers have been added. Usually mixes with organic ingredients are long on carbon compounds and short on nitrogen, which means they need fertilization. In a controlled experiment, researchers with the California Dept. of Agriculture found that commercial planting mixes vary in their ability to support plant growth, even with fertilizers added. There was no way of telling which mediums were best without testing them by growing plants in them.

VERMICULITE - is puffed mica which has been "popped" with heat. It is inert, and holds water like a sponge. It is often mixed with other ingredients to loosen the mix and aid in both its water and air retention. It comes in various sizes. The coarse and medium sizes are preferred because they allow more air to form between the particles than the fine. Vermiculite is very light weight.

CAUTION: **Dry vermiculite produces a lot of dust which is harmful to breathe. It contains minute amounts of asbestos. Before using the material wet it down with water. This prevents the dust from forming. It comes in 4 cubic foot bags at nurseries and grow stores.**

PERLITE - is puffed volcanic pumice. It does not absorb water, but holds it on/in its pitted surface. It is used to loosen planting mixes and stabilize their water holding properties. It is so light weight it floats in water. It comes in various sizes. Coarse perlite allows the most air to mix with the medium.

CAUTION: **Dry perlite produces an obnoxious dust. Wet it down before using it.**

SAND - both construction or horticultural- was much more popular as a soil ingredient before vermiculite and perlite were available. It performs many of the same duties in the planting mix; stabilizing water retention and loosening the structure. The problem with sand is its weight. Even a cupful of sand adds considerable weight to a container.

GRAVEL - holds a little water on its surface and loosens soil. It is heavy and tends to sink in the medium. It is sometimes used alone in hydroponic mixes.

LAVA - holds water on its irregular surface and holes in its structure. It is lighter weight than gravel. It is sometimes used as a hydroponic medium. Clay pellets are sometimes used in place of lava because they are lighter weight. Pea size pieces are the best to use.

STYROFOAM - is hydrophobic, and is used to keep mediums dryer. It is extremely lightweight and tends to float to the surface of the medium. Usually the little balls are used but sometimes irregular chips are.

PEAT MOSS - is chopped and decayed moss. It performs many tasks in planting mixes. It helps to retain water and holds nutrients and is a nutrient buffer which holds excess nutrients rather than letting them remain too concentrated in the water. For this reason most commercial mixes contain peat moss. It is very acidic and will lower the pH of the medium so that it should compose no more than 20% of the mix.

STEER MANURE - is fairly rich in nitrogen and other nutrients including trace elements. It holds water well. Many growers swear by it. Unless it is pasteurized, it may contain insect eggs and other pests.

BARK - is lightweight, absorbs water and holds air in its pores. As it comes in contact with fertilized water it slowly deteriorates, becoming more of a compost. It is used extensively by commercial greenhouse growers. It can be substituted for lava and it weighs much less.

THE SUBSTRATES

Substrates have recently become the hot end of the medium market. These are materials which come in a solid form, usually a block, and need no pre-preparation. They are just placed in the growing chamber and watered. They are inert, sterile and hold water and air well. Most experiments show that plants do better in these mediums than in most mixes. Transplanting substrates is very easy. The smaller used piece is placed on top of the larger new piece. The roots grow into the new block. All of the substrates support fast vigorous growth.

ROCKWOOL - is the most popular substrate. Originally it was used as an insulating material in home construction. Then commercial greenhouse growers in Europe started to use it for their crops. Rockwool looks a lot like fiberglass. It is made by heating rock and extruding it into thin threads. Rockwool comes in pre-pressed blocks and filled bags. It is lightweight and it holds a tremendous amount of water, more than soil, but allows plenty of air in. It comes in several forms, blocks and cubes of various sizes, bags filled with loose fiber and bales of fiber to be placed in containers. It is reuseable for several crops. See photo on page 51.

CAUTION: **Rockwool releases noxious fibers when it is dry. Before growers use rockwool, the material should be wetted. A face mask and rubber or leather gloves, should be used. Body should be covered with a face mask in place.**

FLORAL FOAM - is used to make flower arrangements. It is very lightweight when dry, but holds a tremendous amount of water. It is inert and easy to use. It releases no deleterious fibers into the environment. The

Rockwool provides a uniform consistancy and holds both water and air.

problem with floral foam is that horticultural grades come only in small cubes. The larger blocks which are used for floral arrangements have been treated with a preservative which is not good for growing plants. Before these blocks are used they should be well rinsed with water to remove the chemicals.

FOAM RUBBER - (such as the stuff used for mattresses) is lightweight and holds a lot of water and air. It is inert and easy to use in either the block form or as chips in a container. It can also be added to planting mixes if chopped to pea size.

UPHOLSTERER'S FOAM - is a thin structured foam used for furniture. It comes in rolls and is about ½-¾ inch thick, although it is easily compressed. It holds ample quantities of both water and air. Since it does not come in block form it can be used by rolling it up firmly and placing the cylinder in a container or by holding it together using a rubber band or tape. Growers have reported fantastic results using it.

What Growers Do In The Confusion

All of this information might seem a little confusing. An interested party might ask, "Can't someone just throw some dirt in a pot and plant the seed? What's with all of this complex stuff?" Selecting the right medium is very important to the plant, and the mixes are easy to prepare.

Successful houseplants growers often choose their favorite houseplant mix. Here are some adaptions of popular mixes. The mixes with soil, compost or worm castings contain some nutrients for plants and help to "buffer" the nutrients supplied through the water. Buffering means holding nutrients within the chemical structure so that they are temporarily unavailable. This helps prevent overfertilization.

Organic Mixes

These mixes contain organic ingredients which help to support plant growth and act as a buffer.

1. 4 parts topsoil, 1 part peatmoss, 1 part vermiculite, 1 part perlite. Moist. Contains medium high amounts of nutrients. Best for hand watering systems.

2. 1 part worm castings, 2 parts vermiculite, 1 part perlite. Light weight, high in nutrients.

3. 1 part worm castings, 1 part compost, 1 part topsoil, 2 parts vermiculite, 2 parts perlite, 3 parts styrofoam. Holds high amounts of water and air.

4. 1 part worm castings, 1 part peat moss, 1 part lava, 1 part vermiculite, 1 part perlite, 1 part styrofoam. Good buffering capabilities.

Inorganic Mixes

These mixes contain only sterile, inert ingredients and have no nutrient value.

5. 1 part vermiculite, 1 part perlite.

6. 3 parts vermiculite, 3 parts perlite, 2 parts styrofoam

7. 1 part vermiculite, 1 part perlite, 2 parts styrofoam, 1 part sand, 1 part lava, 1 part peatmoss.

8. Lava, pea sized gravel or small ceramic beads alone or mixed with a little vermiculite.

All of the mixes listed will support a vigorous, fast growing crop. Some growers try several different mixes to see which they like working with.

If I had to choose one medium for cultivation, I would use one of the substrates. I feel they have many advantages: They are easy to prepare (no preparation), distribute water and air well, are easily disposable and promote rapid growth. Their main disadvantage is that they have no buffering abilities so that the plants are more sensitive to over-fertilization. First time growers usually feel more confident with a mix.

Step by Step

1. Several different mixes are sometimes tried at the same time.
   A: Mixes with nutrients supply some of the nutrients required by the plant.
   B: Mixes with organic ingredients "buffer" or chemically bind with fertilizers. They allow the grower a little leeway.
   C: Substrates are convenient to set up. They often require no other containers. They require a little more care than other systems.

2. Enough mix is prepared to fill the containers.

Chapter 12
PH

PH is the measure of acid-alkalinity balance of a solution. It is measured on a scale of 1-14 with 1 being most acidic. 7 is neutral and 14 is most alkaline. Most nutrients are soluble in a limited range of acidity from about 6-7. Should the water become too acid or alkaline, the nutrients dissolved in the water precipitate and become unavailable to the plants. When nutrients are locked up, the plants cannot grow. Typically, a plant growing in an environment with a low pH is very small, often growing only a few inches in several months. Plants growing in a high pH environment will look pale and sickly and also have stunted growth.

Ph is measured using aquarium or garden pH chemical test kits pH paper or a pH meter. pH meters are the most convenient to use. The probe is placed in the water or medium and indicates pH. These items are available at plant stores and hi-tech garden centers and are easy to use.

Once the water is tested gardeners adjust it if it is not in the ideal range of 6.2-6.8. Hydroponic supply companies sell pH adjusters which are convenient and highly recommended. The solution can also be adjusted using common household chemicals. The pH of highly acidic solutions can be raised using bicarbonate of soda, wood ash or hydrated lime. Alkaline water can be adjusted using nitric or sulphuric acid, citric acid or vinegar. Once a standard measure of how much chemical is needed to adjust the water, the process becomes fast and easy to do.

Plants affect the pH of the water solution as they remove various nutrients. Microbes growing in the medium also change the pH. PH is adjusted whenever the water is changed or added. Since the medium and plants affect the water's pH, growers often take a pH reading of the water after it has passed through the system. Water passing through a low pH medium can be adjusted upwards. High pH mediums such as rockwool are often irrigated using low pH water.

Step By Step

1. The water's pH is tested and adjusted whenever the garden is watered.

Chapter 13
WATER SYSTEMS

There are several ways to get water to the plants: from the top by hand watering or using an automatic drip emitter system, from the bottom using a reservoir system or wicks. All of these systems are easily set up and maintained.

THE SIMPLEST

Everybody has watered a plant from the top. Water is poured into the container until the medium is saturated. After saturation, water drains from the container. Sometimes the containers are placed in a tray.

MORE COMPLEX

An automatic system is convenient when the gardener is not around all the time or sometimes forgets to water. The systems are often home-made.

Most grow rooms are in spaces without drainage. Systems in these areas use an enclosed system with either a top or bottom reservoir. Bottom reservoirs store water in a space below the plants, perhaps under the platform. A pump running periodically on a short range timer pushes water from underneath through a series of drip irrigation tubes to the top of each individual container. Excess water drains once the medium is saturated. Drip irrigation set-ups and instructions are available at the local garden supply store. Suitable pumps are sold in garden supply stores as well as tropical fish stores. Short range timers as well as the other supplies are all available at high-tech indoor garden centers. See illustration at bottom of page 58.

Drip irrigation systems with a reservoir above the garden use a sump pump to move water from the collection tray at the bottom of the garden to the reservoir. Water remains in the top reservoir until a valve opens allowing it to flow through the drip emitter tubes to the containers. Automatic valves with timed opening and closing cycles are available at garden supply stores or can be put together using a closed solenoid valve and timer. Valves are available at plumbing supply stores. See illustration at top of page 58 and photo on page 59.

Solenoid
Valve
Timer
Sump
Pump

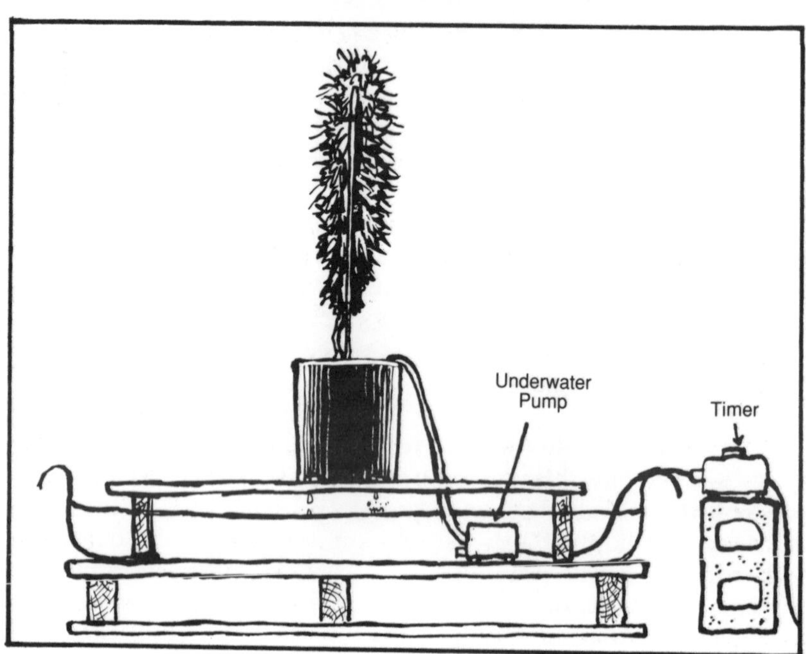
Underwater
Pump
Timer

The plants are irrigated from an overhead reservoir using drip tubing. The water drains onto a sheet of corrugated plastic which drains into a rain gutter and then into a tray. A sump pump recirculates the water back to the reservoir.

Indoor drip emitters are placed over each container, in this case, rockwool.

Gardens situated in a space with water and drain can be constructed using an open system. Water from the tap is supplied to the plants using drip irrigation. Excess water runs out the drain. See photo above.

BACK TO BASICS

The Reservoir System

When plants are watered from the top excess water drains out of the container, and is either captured for re-use or drained away. However, houseplant owners often put a tray under their plants to capture the excess water. The container sits in the water and draws the water as the roots use the water held by the medium.

To assure that the roots oxygen requirements are met, especially the roots which grow into the water, gardeners sometimes place a fishtank air pump with aerator attached which constantly moves the water. Oxygen dissolved in the water is used by the roots.

This system works best with the drier mediums, which are impossible to get too saturated. A mixture of 5 parts lava and 1 part vermiculite is ideal, but mediums which are compact and hold a lot of water in the particles are too moist for this system. Adding a high proportion of lava, gravel or styrofoam pellets helps to dry the medium out.

With the reservoir method the roots sit partially in water. The water level can be up to 20% of the container depth. An 8 inch high container can sit in 1½ inches of water, a 12 inch container can have a water level of 2½ inches. Containers can sit in individual trays, or for convenience of watering they can be placed in a single large tray. Plastic dish trays, lab trays and plastic kiddie pools all make ideal water trays, or a watertight tray one can be constructed from wood coated with plastic resin. See photo below.

Water can be added through the tops of the containers or the water can be poured into the tray. Gardeners use several methods to maintain this system. The water level should be maintained at a constant level by adding water as it is used up.

Most American gardening books advise that when roots sit in water they may be damaged. In Europe however, containers incorporating the reservoir system are sold as standard items in plant stores. As long as the roots come in contact with air containing oxygen, their needs are met.

A ball valve similar to the ones used in toilets are sometimes used to automate this system. When the water level falls, the valve opens up filling the tray to the desired height. When several trays are being used, the valve sits in its own container and controls the water level of all the other containers. The containers are connected to the central unit using tubes. A constant level of water is maintained. See illustration on page 62 and photos on pages 63 and 64.

This is the easiest system to set up. A container with a well drained mix is placed in the tray and water is added.

WATER LINE

This simple unit is very effective and will produce about the same yield as a sophisticated, water moving system.

These simple units increase the time between watering by several days. They add water to the reservoir only as it is needed.

THE WICK SYSTEM

The very first hydroponic units I ever used were wick systems. They consisted of two plastic containers which fit into each other. The bottom of the top container had been drilled and 3¼" thick pieces of nylon cord were strung across the bottom and hung down into the lower container from both sides. The top container was filled with vermiculite. The bottom container was used as a reservoir and the nylon cord drew up water into the vermiculite and kept it moist. The unit produced some incredible vegetables and flowers. Wick systems are very easy to construct, work well and are trouble free. Moist mixes are suitable for this unit. The wicks act as a self-regulating moisture supplier. It is often used by novice growers because it is hard to make a mistake using this system.

There are several ways to automate the wick system. Probably the easiest way is by placing the containers on a platform above a water tray and let the wicks dangle into the water. One grower took a kiddie pool and placed a pallet inside. The containers rested on the pallet. A flush valve system as described for the reservoir system easily automates these units. See illustrations on page 66.

THE EBB AND FLOW OR FLOOD SYSTEM

The flood system is the method most people picture when hydroponics is mentioned. The containers are periodically flooded and then drained. Construction of a manual unit is easy. Imagine a tray with a flexible drain tube on the bottom. The tube is held up in the "plug" position. Water pours into the tray until the containers are flooded. The reservoir, often a water jug, is placed back into position so that it can catch the drain water. Then the tube is placed back into the "drain" position.

Growers often make small automated units. First they seal the reservoir tightly. Two tubes are attached using a bottle stopper. One is attached to an air pump at the other end and pushes air into the top of the reservoir. The other tube goes into the bottom of the reservoir. When the air is pushed into the reservoir the water rises, flooding the growing area. When the pump is turned off, the water flows back to the reservoir. More sophisticated units have a back-flow valve. Usually gardens are flooded twice a day using a short range timer. Larger systems use a water pump to flood the growing area. See illustration on page 67 and photo on page 68.

After each flooding additional water is added to the reservoir to replace the liquid absorbed by the containers.

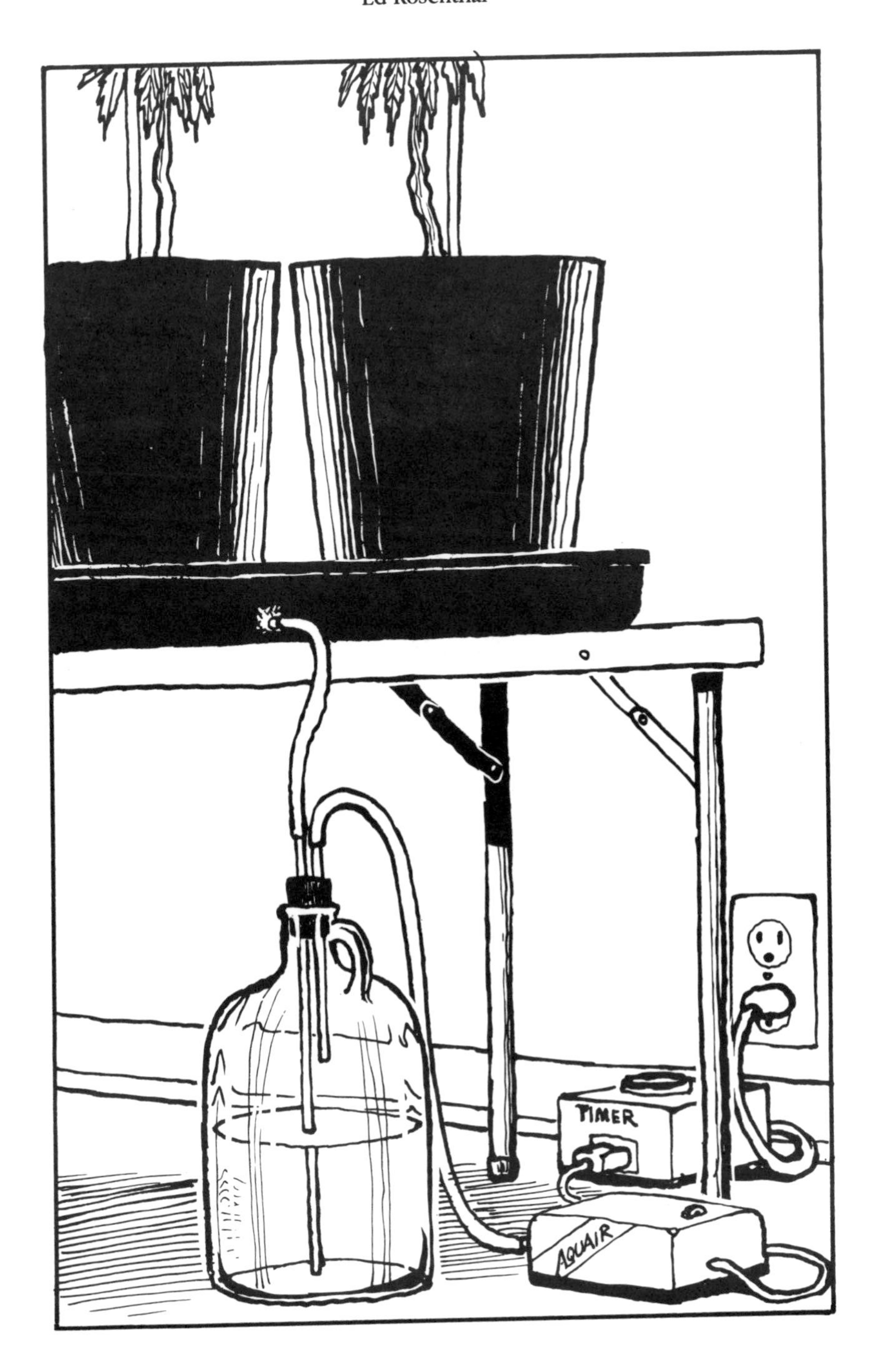
TIMER
AQUAIR

Before watering the drain hole in the tray is plugged. Water is added to the two and one half inch level, then the plug is pulled allowing the water to drain into the holding tank. The grower watered two to three times a day.

Ebb and flow tables are commercially available. These work like the flood system, but only partially submerge the growing container with 2 or 3 inches of water.

Step By Step

1. Gardeners choose the system that they feel is right for themselves. All of the systems work well because they supply the roots everything they need.

The choices are:

A. Watering from the top and letting it drain out.
B. Drip irrigation and letting the water drain out.
C. Automated drip irrigation.
D. Manual reservoir system
E. Automated reservoir system.
F. Aerated water system.
G. Wick system.
H. Automated wick system.
I. Manual flood system.
J. Automated flood system.

All of these systems are designed to support fast growth. The choice is based on convenience.

Chapter 14

NUTRIENTS and FERTILZING

Plants require nutrients in order to grow. The roots absorb the nutrients from the water as dissolved salts. These are the simple compounds found in chemical fertilizers. Organic fertilizers travel a more circuitous route, first breaking down from complex molecules through microbial action, and then dissolving into the water.

Nitrogen (N), Phosphorous (P) and Potassium (K) are called the macro-nutrients because plants use large quantities of them. The percentages of N, P and K are always listed in the same order (N-P-K) on fertilizer packages.

Calcium (Ca), sulfur (S), and magnesium (Mg) are also required in fairly large quantities. They are often called secondary nutrients.

Smaller amounts of iron (Fe), zinc (Zn), manganese (Mn), boron (B), cobalt (Co), copper (Cu), molybdenum (Mo), and chlorine (Cl) are also required. These are called the micro-nutrients.

When marijuana germinates, it requires a modest amount of N and larger amounts of P. This supports vigorous root growth and limits etoliation (stretching) of the stem. When it goes into its vigorous growth stage, usually within two weeks, marijuana's need for N increases. The nutrient is used in building amino acids, the stuff protein is made from. During the reproductive stage, when the plant flowers, the female's flower growth is promoted by P and K.

Plants which are being grown in soil mixes or mixes with nutrients added such compost, worm castings or manure do better when watered with a dilute soluble fertilizer, too. When a non-nutritive medium is used, the nutrients are supplied as a solution in the water from the beginning.

Typical formulas used for the seedling and earlygrowth stages include: 7-9-5, 5-10-5, 4-5-3. Formulas for the fast growth stage usually have a little more nitrogen. Most growers use different formulas for the different growth stages. Other growers supplement low nitrogen formulas with fish emulsion or other high nitrogen formulas. Some gardeners use the same fertilizers throughout the plant's life cycle. A typical formula for this is 20-20-20.

Plants growing under warm conditions (over 80 degrees) are given less N to prevent stem etoliation. Plants grown in cool environments are given more N.

During flowering a high P formula promotes flower growth. Formulas such as 3-10-4, 5-20-5 and 4-30-12 are used. Plants are sometimes grown using a nutrient solution containing no N for the last 10 days. Many of the larger leaves yellow and wither as N migrates from old to new growth.

The fertilizer should be complete, that is, it should contain all of the secondary and trace elements. Some fertilizers do not contain Mg. This is supplemented using Epsom salts, available at drug stores. Sometimes growers prefer to use more than one fertilizer. They find that changing the formulas and ingredients helps to prevent stresses and deficiencies. However, the chemicals in each fertilizer are blended to remain soluble. Different fertilizer formulas may react with each other. As a result some of the chemicals may precipitate and become unavailable to the plants. To prevent this growers use only one fertilizer at each watering.

Overfertilization is a very dangerous. When plants are under-fertilized more nutrient can be added, no harm done. Overfertilization can kill a plant quickly.

Grower take no chances when they change hydroponic nutrient-water solutions every 2 weeks. Even though the solution may have nutrients left, it is probably unbalanced since the plants have used some of the nutrients, and not others.

Chapter 15
AIR AND TEMPERATURE

Temperature, movement, humidity and content of the air all affect plant growth.

Unlike warm-blooded animals, which can function regardless of the outside temperature, plants' rate of metabolism, how fast they function and grow is controlled by the temperature of the surrounding air.

At low temperatures, under 65 degrees, the photosynthesis rate and growth are slowed. The difference in growth rate is not readily apparent if the temperature dips once in a while or the low temperatures are not extreme. However, temperatures under 50-55 degrees virtually stop growth. Temperatures in the 40's cause slight temporary tissue damage. When temperatures dip into the high thirties tissue damage which takes several days to repair may result, especially in older plants.

When temperatures rise above 78 degrees, cannabis' rate of growth slows once again as the plant uses part of its energy to dissipate heat and keep its water content constant. The rate of growth continues to slow as the temperature rises. Photosynthesis and growth stop somewhere in the 90's.

When the lights are off, photosynthesis stops. Instead, the plants use the sugars and starches for energy and tissue building. The plants do best when the temperature is lower during this part of the cycle. The fact that the lamps are off, will lower the temperature quite a bit, and ventilation can be used to cool the space down.

Looking at a marijuana leaf under a magnifying glass, a viewer will notice that there are small "hairs" covering it. These appendages form a windbreak which slows air movement around the leaf. This helps to modify the temperature by holding air which has been warmed by the tissue surface, similar to the way hair or fur keeps warm air trapped near the skin.

Since plants transpire water, the air surrounding the leaf surfaces is more humid than the air in the surrounding environment.

Outside, there is usually a breeze so that air is ventilated from the surface. The breeze removes waste gasses and humidity and brings fresh air containing CO_2 in contact with the surface.

Indoors, air movement is easily achieved using fans. The movement should be swift but not forceful. Leaves should have slight movement. Oscillating fans are convenient means gardeners use to provide an air stream to all sections of the garden. A draft which is too strong can be buffered against a wall so that the current reaches the garden indirectly.

Marijuana functions best at a humidity of 40-65%. Higher humidity causes problems in two ways. First, fungi which attack marijuana become active at higher humidities. They affect all parts of the plant, but especially the buds, which contain moisture holding crevices, are dark and have little air movement. The other problem with high humidity is that plants have a hard time dissipating water transpired by the stomata (plant pores).

The humidity level is a measure of how saturated the air is with moisture. That is, how much water the air is holding as a percentage of its water holding potential. The warmer the air the more moisture it can absorb, so that when the temperature rises the air becomes less saturated and the humidity goes down, even though the same amount of water is dissolved in the air. The reverse happens when the temperature declines. The same amount of water may be in the air, but the air's water holding capacity is lower so the humidity rises.

There are several ways to maintain the proper temperature and humidity. The easiest method gardeners use to rid a space of excess heat or moisture is to vent the space. Small spaces such as a closet or shelf are easily vented into the room because of the large surface area in contact with the general space. Room temperature and humidity conditions are similar to those needed by the plants. Heated rooms may be a little low in humidity, but the moisture level in the micro-environment surrounding the plants is usually higher. This is caused by evaporation of water from the medium and by plant transpiration.

Since hot air rises and cool air sinks, a fan placed above the plants pulls out the heated air. Squirrel fans and other ventilation fans make these set-ups a snap. Experienced gardeners choose fans with the capacity to move the room's cubic area every 10 minutes. As an example a fan in 200 cubic foot grow space moved 20 cubic feet per minute.

Increasing the rate of air change using a fan has beneficial effects besides controlling temperature and humidity. A breeeze which causes some movement of the stem increases its strength. When a plant moves in the wind, small tears develop in the tissues. The plant quickly grows new tissue, thickening and strengthening the stem. A breeze also increases the amount of CO_2 available to the plant. This is covered in depth in chapter 17- CO_2.

Sensible growers know that open windows are not as good a solution as fans for several reasons. They present a new problem regarding detection, both by light and odor, and plant pests living outside might use the passageway to find new indoor feeding grounds.

Some growers use a closed system. The air is cooled using an air conditioner, the humidity is lowered using a dehumidifier and the CO_2 is supplied using a tank. Each of these units is connected to a sensor so that they go on and off automatically. In temperate areas the air conditioner remains only a small part of the time, except during the summer when it may be called on for heavy duty work. The air conditioner also dehumidifies the room. A small sized dehumidifier can keep a room at desired humidity when the temperature is within the acceptable range.

Grow spaces located in basements or attics may get cool during the winter. An electric or gas heater designed for indoor use is often used to increase the temperature. Electric heaters raise the temperature, but decrease the humidity of the room because no additional moisture is added to the air. Gas heaters vented into the grow space provide CO_2, moisture and heat to the plants.

Plant roots are very sensitive to cold temperatures. Containers placed directly on a cold floor lose their heat. To conserve warmth the units are set on a pallet or the floor, or it is covered with a layer of styrofoam sheet, which is both an excellent insulation material and light reflector. Heat mats and heating cables which are thermostatically regulated to keep trays and soil in the mid-seventies are sold in many garden shops. Water in reservoirs is often heated using aquarium equipment.

Chapter 16
CARBON DIOXIDE

Carbon dioxide (CO_2) is a colorless, odorless gas found in the air. Under normal circumstances, including the conditions growers deal with, it is totally harmless. Each molecule consists of one part carbon and two parts oxygen. CO_2 is often generated in the home. When a stove or water heater burns gas it produces water vapor and CO_2.

Plants use CO_2 as a raw material during the process of photosynthesis. CO_2 is quickly used up in a well lit enclosed space. Until it is replaced, the process cannot continue. The availability of CO_2 to the plant can be a limiting factor in photosynthesis and plant growth.

Keeping the door or curtain of a small grow room open helps tremendously because a whole side of the grow space is exposed to external air. An open door in a large a room gives a much smaller ratio of interface, since the percentage of the perimeter serving as a vent is much smaller.

CO_2 constitutes about .03%, or 300 parts per million of air in country areas and about .035-.04% in industrialized regions. Photosynthesis and growth could proceed at a much higher rate if the amount of CO_2 available were increased to about .15% or 1500 parts per million instead of the .035-.04% found in urban areas. Higher concentrations of CO_2 can increase the growth rate up to 300%. Usually though, growers report increases of under 100%. Either way, growth rate is increased significantly. When plants grow faster, it takes less time to yield a bigger crop. Once CO_2 enrichment is added to the grow space, light will most likely be the limiting factor.

The most practical method that a closet farmer has to enrich the garden with gas is a CO_2 tank with a regulator. The regulators are sold by all of the high-tech garden supply companies. These devices control the number of cubic feet of gas released to the garden. CO_2 gas refills are available from companies listed under the Bottled Gas or Industrial Gas sections of the Yellow Pages. The largest tanks hold 50 pounds of gas, but they weigh 170 pounds filled. A 20 pound tank is much smaller and weighs about 50 pounds filled. At room temperature there are 8.7 cubic feet in a pound of gas. Refills are inexpensive.

CO_2 enrichment reduces ventilation requirements considerably for several reasons. First, the CO_2 in the air is being replenished and the plants function more efficiently at a higher temperature when CO_2 is at high levels. Rather than trying to draw in CO_2 from the surrounding atmosphere, the aim is now to stop the gas from dispersing into it.

Growers figure out how much gas to use by finding the number of cubic feet (ft^3) there are in the grow space (Length x Width x Height). For instance, a closet 6 feet long, 2.5 feet wide and 8.5 feet high contains 127.5 ft^3. Then they multiply that number by .0015. In this case the figures look like this: 127.5 x .0015=.191 ft^3.

One grower had a closet 3 feet by 3 feet by 10 feet. He figured that its area was 90 ft^3. To find the amount of gas to inject he multiplied 90 x .0015= .135 ft^3.

For each one hundred ft^3 of space about .15 ft^3 of gas is required.

1 lb. CO_2= 8.7 cubic feet

Small unventilated closet areas are sometimes set up with a constant flow of CO_2 enrichment when the lights are on. Well designed ventilated rooms are re-enriched every time the ventilation stops. Unventilated rooms need a full replenishment of CO_2 every one to two hours.

A room 6 x 3 x 9=162 ft^3. The lights are on continuously and the air is enriched with a steady flow of .25 ft^3 of CO_2 per hour. Six feet of gas is used per day. A 20 lb. tank holds 20 x 8.7= 174 ft^3 ÷ 6 = 29 days of use per refill.

Growers often ventilate the hot air out of the space to disperse heat. They found that it does not do much for the plants to run the CO_2 enrichment system and the ventilation system at the same time, since the gas is drawn out. Instead, the CO_2 unit goes on after the ventilation system has stopped and quickly re-innoculates the area with CO_2. Some high-tech garden companies sell devices designed to regulate the systems automatically.

CO_2 is heavier than air, and when it comes out of the tank it is being depressurized, which makes it cold. Subsequently, the gas sinks as it enters the space. In gardens with little internal ventilation the tubing is usually suspended just over the tops of plants. In large spaces the gas is sometimes dispersed using laser drilled irrigation tubing or released in front of the internal fans.

Exhaust gas emitted from a stove or water heater is suitable for the garden. A garden in a room with a water heater will be enriched every time the burners light. Of course, anytime a person works with natural or LP gas or with fire, they must be very careful. See photo below.

Step By Step

Plants do best in indoor gardens when they are supplied with CO_2. Growers usually choose:

1. An open door or curtain is often the best solution for small spaces which have a large surface-to-air ratio.
2. External ventilation to blow out the used air and draw in new air. This is usually adequate for small rooms.
3. A CO_2 enrichment system. This consists of a tank and regulator-flow meter and either a timer or other automatic valve. This increases the growth rate of the plants phenomonally.
4. A water heater or gas stove may supplement the garden with CO_2.

A CO_2 tank and regulator is used to enrich the air. CO_2 laden air increases the growth rate phenomenally.

Chapter 17

ODOR and IONS

Odors are caused by minute solids floating in the air. Each particle has a positive electrical charge because it is missing an electron. This enables it to drift as it is drawn in one direction and then another by electrical charges.

There are several ways growers eliminate these particles. Air filters use filter pads and activated charcoal to cleanse the air. More sophisticated units also use electrostatic precipitators to remove minute particles. These units have a negatively charged lining which attracts any positively charged particles passing through.

The easiest and most effective method gardeners use eliminate odors is using a negative ion generator. These units are sometimes called ion fountains or air ionizers. Negative ion generators charge air molecules with extra electrons, giving them a negative charge. When negatively charged air ions comes in contact with a positively charged dust particle, the air molecule gives up its electron. The positively charged particle is neutralized and no longer floats since it is not as influenced by electrical charges. The particle drops from the air (precipitates) and falls onto the wall or floor. It no longer creates an odor.

Negative ion generators are inexpensive and cost very little to operate. They solve the most daunting odor problems. In addition, ionizers precipitate dust.

A number of studies have shown that the electrical charge of the air influences behavior in animals and growth in plants. Negatively charged air seems to be conducive to less irritable behavior in animals and faster growth in plants. See photo on page 82.

These units release negative ions which precipitate solids including odor particles.

Chapter 18

SETTING UP

Before a seed is planted or a cutting transferred to the new garden, successful growers make sure the space is ready. All lights, timers, water and ventilation systems should be working. The space should be lined with reflective material so that all light is directed to the growing area. Units in which water is transported are thoroughly tested and adjusted so that there is no flooding, and so the pumps work when they are supposed to.

The Medium

Ingredients are mixed in buckets or a large tray. Larger amounts are more easily mixed using a cement mixer or a shovel in a large space. The mix is added to the container to a level ¾-1 inch below the top. After adding the mix, the container is watered again so that the mix settles.

Substrates are placed in position and thoroughly watered.

CAUTION: **Planting medium dust is harmful to breathe. Intelligent growers have been seen to moisten all the ingredients of with a watering can or hose before mixing. This prevents dust from getting into the air. This is extremely important since respiratory problems have been associated with dust.**

No matter what kind of system is being used, experienced growers try a final test run. They make sure that delivery and drainage lines are working properly and that the units are receiving the right amounts of water in the right places. Pumps and timers are carefully inspected to make sure they are working properly. It is much easier to repair the system before the plants are growing.

Wall areas likely to receive light are painted reflective white or lined with reflective materials so that any light missing the garden area is reflected back to it.

The ventilation fans must be working properly. The goal is to supply a steady stream of air to the plants without the space being drafty.

Finally, the system is run for a day to make sure that all of the components are working in a coordinated fashion. The outside ventilation should be regulated by a thermostat or timer so the room stays in the 70's during the light cycle. When the fans go off, CO_2 should be released. Automatic irrigation systems should keep the medium well moistened.

When everything is working, it is time for the grower to plant. See photo on page 85.

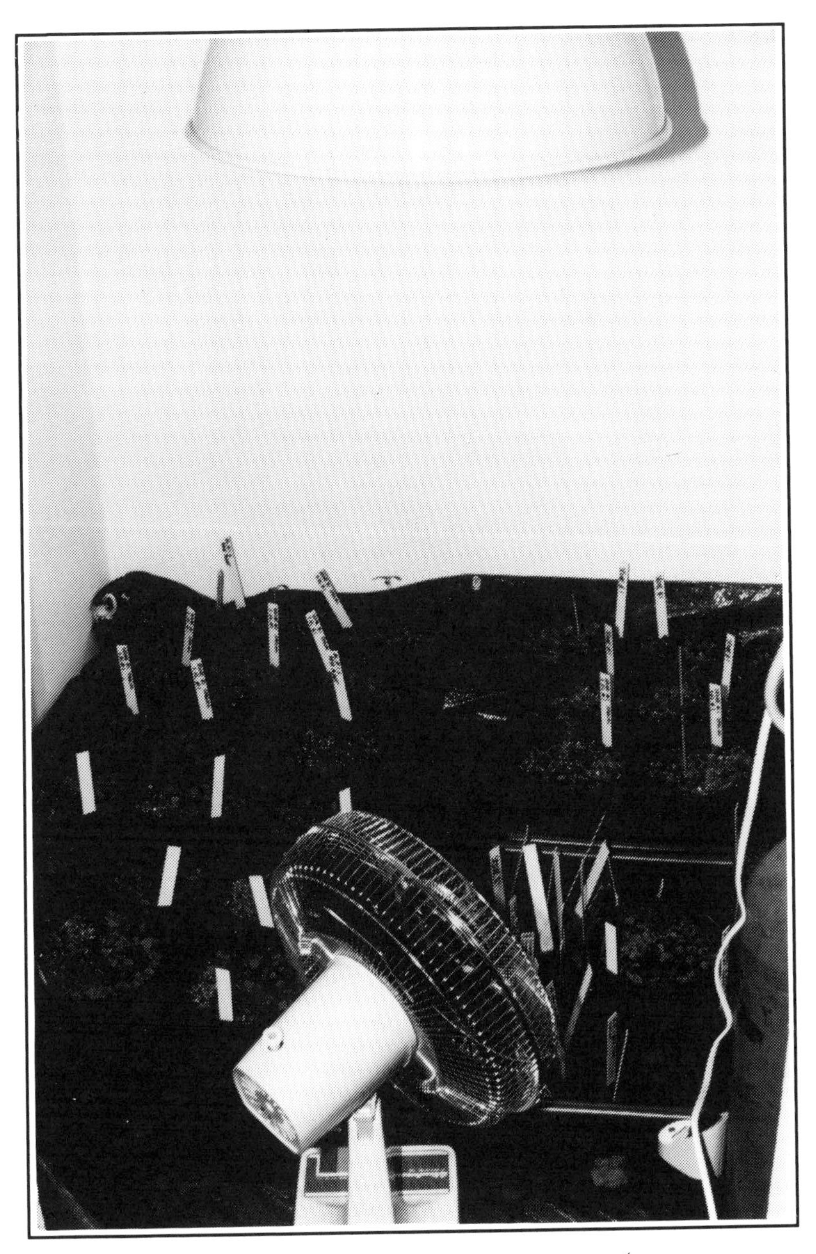

These trays were planted with seed about five days ago. They will be harvested in 100 days.

Chapter 19
PLANTING

Successful growers plant marijuana seeds about a half inch deep and then cover them. Seeds placed in substrates are pushed into the material so that they are totally surrounded. Once the seeds are planted, the medium is watered again to help the seeds settle in place. The direction that the seed faces is not important. Using gravity as a means of sensing proper direction, the seed will direct roots downward and the stem upward.

Marijuana need not be planted in its final container to start. Even a plant which is destined to be a giant can be started in a 2 inch pot or block. The advantage to starting small is that the plants do not take up unneeded room. However, plants must be given more room soon after germination or they will become rootbound, which stunts the plants. Seedlings are transplanted using the same techniques described under cuttings.

Germination begins when moisture seeps through the seed coat and signals the seed to start growing. Heat regulates the rate of germination and growth until the seedling reaches light.

Water

The planting medium is kept moist until germination is complete. If the surface of the medium tends to dry out, plastic wrap is placed over it to retain moisture.

Seedlings have tender root systems which are easily damaged when the medium dries out so the medium is kept moist at all times.

Heat

Marijuana germinates rapidly when the planting medium is kept at an even temperature. Room temperature, about 70 degrees, is best. When the medium is cool, germination slows and the seeds may be attacked by fungi or other organisms. With high temperatures, seedlings grow thin and spindly, especially under low light conditions. This occurs because their growth rate is sped up by the heat, but the seedlings are not photosynthesizing enough sugar for use as building material.

Light

Once the seedling breaks ground and comes in contact with light, it starts to photosynthesize, thus producing its own food for growth. When the light is dim, the plant stretches to reach it. In the wild the seedling is in competition with other plants which may be shading it. By growing taller it may be able to reach unobstructed light. However, a stretched seedling is weaker than one with a shorter but thicker stem and has a tendency to fall over. Seedlings with ample light grow squat, thick stems. Seedlings can be started in constant bright light of the same intensity that is to be used for their growth cycle.

Some growers recommend that seeds be germinated in a napkin or on a sponge and then placed into the growing area. This method risks damage to the seedling in many ways; the delicate plant tissues may be damaged by handling or moisture problems, the seedlings are more likely to be attacked by infections and they may be subject to delays in growth caused by changes in their position in relation to gravity. See photos on pages 89, 90 and 91.

CUTTINGS (CLONES)

Many growers populate their gardens with cuttings rather than seeds. Cuttings have several advantages over seeds. These are discussed in Chapter 27, Clones. Transplanting cuttings is very easy.

Cuttings which have been rooted in a substrate such as floral foam, Jiffy rooting cubes or rockwool are easily placed in a larger rooting area. If the cuttings are being transferred to another substrate, the small block with the rooted cutting can be placed firmly on top of the larger substrate. Growers rub the two blocks together so that there is firm contact between the two materials. The roots will grow directly from the smaller block into the larger one.

Growers report that it is also easy to transplant substrate rooted cuttings into a soil or soil-less medium. The cutting is not held by the leaf or stem, because the pull of the heavy block may injure the stem or tear the roots. Instead, the block is held and placed in a partially filled container. After placing the block in the container, mix is placed around it so that the block is totally covered. The medium is tapped down firmly enough so that it is well packed but not tight or compacted.

When transplanting plants grown in degradable containers such as peat pots or Jiffy cubes, growers report best results when the containers are cut in several places. This assures an easy exit for the roots.

DAY 1. Germination. The cotyledon, the first leaves of the plant open, and start photosynthetic food production.

DAY 2 - 3. The first set of true leaves appear.

DAY 3 - 5. A second set of leaves has opened and the third and fourth sets have opened. Vigorous growth is about to begin.

Cuttings growing in individual containers are transplanted before they are root-bound. First, the rootball is knocked from the container. To do this, growers turn the plant upside down so that the top of the soil is resting between the index and middle finger of one hand with the stem of the plant sticking through the fingers. The container is held in the other hand and knocked against a hard surface such as a table. The rootball is jarred loose from the old container and rests in the gardener's hand. The rootball is placed in a larger container partially filled with mix. Then mix is added to bring the medium to within a half inch of the top of the pot. When plants have a long bare stem, growers sometimes place the plant deeply in the container, burying part of the stem. See illustrations on page 93.

Paper cups are sometimes used as containers. They are carefully opened using a utility knife or scissors. Rootballs sticking to styrofoam cups sometimes release if the cup is rolled tightly between two palms before knocking. If the rootball still sticks, the cup is cut open.

Once the rootball is out it is placed in a container partially filled with medium. More medium is added packed firmly around the rootball, until the top is covered.

Transplants sometimes take a few days to adjust. Then their growth spurts with renewed vigor.

Step By Step

1. Seeds are usually planted one half inch deep and covered.
2. Growers often start seeds in smalll containers. They are transplanted as they grow. This way small plants do not waste unused space.
3. Seeds are kept moist at 70 (degrees) to encourage fast germination.
4. Growers transplant cuttings easily by placing the the rootball in a partially filled container. Then planting medium is added until the ball is completely covered.

Chapter 20
VEGETATIVE GROWTH

Growers report that once the seeds have sprouted, the plants begin a period of fast growth. With good conditions plants grow three or four sets of leaves within the first 10 days. After that they really take off, growing both top and side branches. By the end of the first month, a stocky plant usually grows between one and one and a half feet. After two months of growth plants grow between two and three feet depending on conditions and variety. Plants grown using intense light and CO_2 grow faster.

Rooted cuttings in an adequate size container grow very quickly, usually faster than seedlings for the first few weeks. Clones develop a stockier stem, with shorter internodes and their branching patterns may also be different from their sisters grown from seed.

Light

During vegetative growth the plants do best when the lights are kept on continuously. The plants do not need a "rest period." Some growers cut the expense of running high watt lamps 24 hours a day by turning them off for 1-6 hours. However, costs other than light, such as rent, labor and risk remain fixed no matter what the light cycle is set at. This means that the garden is at maximum efficiency on a continuous light cycle. It actually costs growers more to grow an ounce of bud using an 18 hour cycle rather than a continuous one. Of course, meter considerations may dictate a break in the light period.

Water

The medium is kept moist continuously. Reservoir and wick hydroponic systems are self regulating; the medium draws water from the reservoir to maintain an even level of moisture. However, the reservoirs must be refilled periodically. Large plants use more water than small ones, so their reservoirs are checked more often. Once the reservoir is filled with water-nutrient mix, added water is clear, pH adjusted and nutrient free.

Active hydroponic systems require irrigation two to four times a day. Warm gardens with large plants use more water than cool gardens with small plants. Reservoirs of re-circulating systems are refilled with pH adjusted nutrient-free water after each irrigation.

Plants growing in soil-type mixes also must be kept moist.

Small plants in a cool space may not need water for 4 or 5 days. Larger plants in a warm space may require irrigation daily, especially if they are kept in small containers.

When watering most growers irrigate until the containers drain. Cold water can shock the roots and hot water can burn them. They do best when irrigated with lukewarm water, in the low 70's.

Nutrients

Smart growers know that fertilizers are best used as directed. The worst thing that a gardener can do is overfertilize, since this can cause the plants' sudden death. The nutrient-water solution is changed every other week. The old water is drained and replaced with fresh nutrient-water solution. The system need not be rinsed. The old water is suitable for use in the outdoor garden. See photos on page 97.

Plant at 10 days

Plant at 20 days

Plant at 30 days

Plant at 40 days

Chapter 21
FLOWERING

The goal of the closet cultivator is to grow plants which yield a large crop of sinsemilla, the unfertilized female flowers of the plant. Usually male and female flowers grow on separate plants. By removing the male plants from the garden, the females remain unpollinated. Pollinated plants put much of their energy into producing seeds, rather than bud growth.

Unpollinated plants grow clusters of flowers over a period of 4 to 8 weeks. Within a few weeks the growth takes the shape of a bud. As the buds ripen, the clusters of flowers grow thicker and the resin glands found on the small leaves and branches begin to swell as they fill up with THC. When it is ripe, the bush fluoresces with 10,000 points of light.

When to Flower

Indoors, growers force marijuana to flower at any time. Even seedlings will indicate sex and produce flowers given the right conditions.

Marijuana flowers in response to the light cycle. Under natural conditions, the plant senses oncoming autumn by chemically measuring the uninterrupted dark period. Indoors, when the light regimen includes a dark period of 10-12 hours each day, the plant stops its vegetative growth cycle and starts growing reproductive organs, male and female flowers, which usually occur on separate plants.

When light hits a leaf, the tissue absorbs certain rays which it uses in photosynthesis. Those rays are unavailable to leaves below the top. 1000 watt HID lights penetrate only 12-18 inches of leaves depending on their size and quantity. Vegetative material below this canopy receives little light, does little photosynthesizing and produces little energy for the plant.

Since a tall plant produces no larger a than a short one, the plants are forced to flower when they are 8-15 inches tall. At maturity they will stand only 18-36 inches.

When the light cycle is switched to "short day," the plant's growth changes from vegetative- the production of leaves and stems, to the reproductive cycle. A few days after the change in the light regimen, all visible growth slows down. Then the first flowers appear.

Males usually indicate first. Using a photographer's loupe or a magnifying glass, the immature male flowers can be differentiated from the females. They look like small pawnbrokers balls hanging from a stem, or a small cluster of grapes. The mature flowers have 5 very small white or yellow petals and a lot of pollen.

The immature female flowers are oval, pointed up and have a very thin hair-like strand extending from each flower. These strands are called pistils and when they pick up pollen which is floating in the air, the flower is pollinated.

As soon as any male plants indicate sex, before the flowers open, growers remove them from the garden. This prevents the females from being fertilized. See illustration on page 101 and photos on pages 102-108.

Here are the stages of flower growth.

1. Slowdown then stop of vegetative growth. 4-10 days after beginning forcing. Lasts up to a week.

2. Appearance of first flowers. 10 days to 15 days after beginning forcing.

3. Massive growth of flowers at the budding sites. Continuing after the first appearance of flowers for 30 to 40 days. During this time the buds develop and take shape. Starting with a few flowers, layer after layer of flowers is grown until the bud sites are merged together into one large cola.

4. Maturation. Eventually the pistils start to turn color from pale white to red or brown. At the same time the flowers close up, forming false seed pods. The small glands on the flowers now start to grow. These are called stalked capitate glands and are composed of a tiny stalk supporting a thin clear membrane. As THC is produced near the site, the membrane swells with the potent liquid. The membrane stretches and the gland takes on the appearance of a mushroom. When the glands have swelled and the pistil has receded into the false pod, the bud is ready to pick.

At the point of maturity, the cola almost glows. This is caused by light hitting the tiny glands filled with THC. The bud looks like a flower which has jewels scattered all over.

The number of days from onset of flowering to maturity varies depending on variety and the length of the dark period. The shorter the dark period, the faster the flowers mature. However, when the flowers are

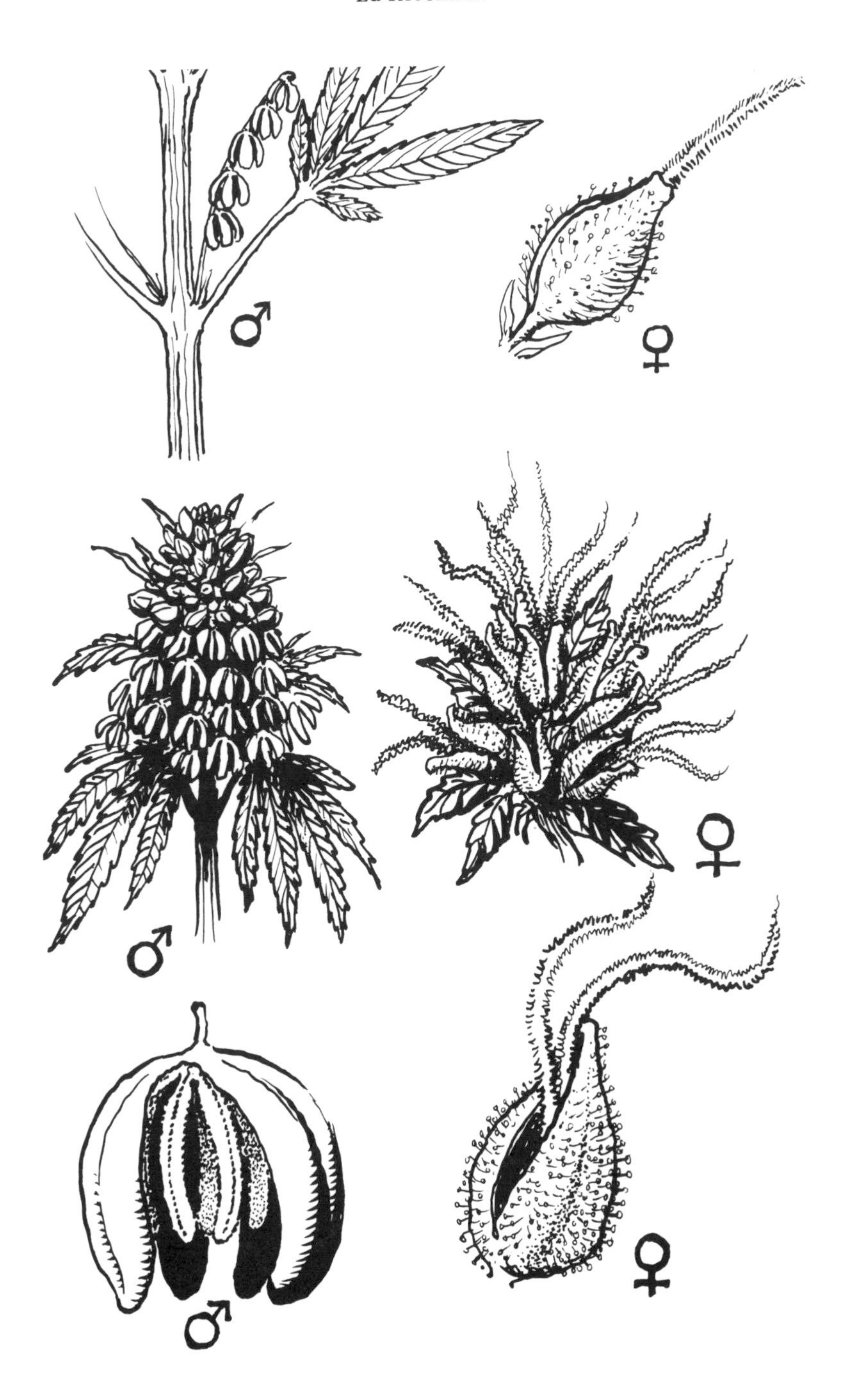

Vegetative growth has stopped and several pistils have grown.

The tops of each branch are begining to erupt with the simple female flowers.

Masses of pistils stretch from the branches seeking pollen. It is apparent that the plant is putting all its energy into flower production. The resin glands are beginning to fill up and are beginning to fill with resin.

brought to maturity faster, they are smaller than when they are given more time to mature. For instance, a bud under a regimen of 12 hours of darkness may take 6 weeks to mature. The same bud, kept under a 14 hour darkness regimen may take only five weeks to mature but may weigh 15% less than the longer maturing bud.

Some growers start the flowering cycle at 10-12 hours of darkness. After 4 weeks they turn up the dark part of the cycle to 14-16 hours of darkness and the buds quickly mature.

Sometimes parts of the bud are mature but new growth is continuing. Most growers pick when the rate of this growth slows. However, the mature parts of the bud can be removed using a small pair of scissors. Some varieties respond to pruning by continuing to produce new growth.

A few varieties including Thai and other South East Asian plants are natural hermaphrodites which produce flowers intermittantly under a 12 hour regimen. They have adapted to the latitude in Thailand which is close to the Equator and does not have much seasonal variation of daylight hours. Colombian varieties have also adapted to low latitude conditions by prolonging flowering a bit, until it catches up with a chronological schedule.

The flowers are very dense and new growth is making the bud tight and heavy. The bud's diameter is increasing daily. There are resin glands covering the entire flower area. They have filled enough to glow under a bright light.

The entire area is covered with glands. There is just a little new growth. The pistils are beginning to dry up and change color from white to orange, red or purple shades. The resin glands are swelling.

Virtually all of the pistils have dried. The glands are swollen with THC and have an irridesence under a bright light.

"SEEDED BUD"
Each flower has swollen with a seed. The pistils seem to be withdrawing into the seed pods. The pods are covered with glands swollen with THC. The bracts are beginning to open, revealing mature seeds.

Chapter 22
DRYING

Some growers point out that a few buds are easily dried by placing them in a loosely folded brown paper bag at room temperature. Larger amounts are hung or placed on trays in a dark area such as a closet. The buds need some air circulation and have a relatively high humidity, so that they dry fairly slowly. It is reported that bud dried for 2-5 days smokes much smoother than it does when it is dried quickly. The reason is that after picking, the buds are still alive and some of the chlorophyll and starch is used by the dying cells.

Some growers use a microwave or oven to dry the buds. Microwaves do not hurt the THC, but marijuana dried this way has a harsh taste as compared to the slow dried. Growers microwave by placing a wet bud in the oven for 30 second periods until it is smokeable. After seeing how long the sample takes to dry, the grower sets the timer for a minute less than the total time used on the sample so the grass does not get crispy.

Oven drying is riskier. If the temperature is too warm, the THC evaporates and is totally lost, so the oven is kept at a low temperature, and should not go above 150 degrees. Hemp kept in the oven too long comes out crisp and stale.

Electric dehydrators are safe to use, but once again, the hemp is dried very quickly and has a harsher, green taste, than when it is dried over a longer period of time. Cannabis connoisseurs do not recommend solar dehydrators. Sunlight reduces the potency of drying buds.

Buds drying on a line.

Chapter 23
CUTTINGS AND CLONES

Nearly everyone has taken a cutting from a houseplant and placed it in water. Within a short time roots grew and the new plant was ready to be placed in a container with medium. The new plant had the same genetic make-up of its clone mother. The new plant's growth, flowers, and reactions to environment were exactly the same as the plant from which it was taken.

The genetic make-up, and therefore the characteristics of a plant started from seed cannot be determined until the plant is grown. Although the lineage of the plant may provide a fair amount of information, there is no way of pre-determining its exact qualities. There are literally billions of possible combinations of genes that the two parents can supply. No two plants from seed are likely to be identical.

There are many advantages to growing genetically identical plants. Here are some which growers have brought to my attention:

1. The plants have uniform growth characteristics so the garden is easier to maintain. Each plant grows to the same size, has approximately the same yield and matures at the same time as its sisters. Starting from seeds, plants of the same variety exhibit subtle differences in growth patterns.

2. Buds from clone sisters will be of the same potency and taste the same.

3. There will be no males in the garden. Since all clones from a single "clone-mother" have the same genetic make-up, clones from a female plant can be only female. Usually about half of the plants from seeds turn out to be male. Using clones saves valuable garden space which would have been used to grow males.

4. Clones seem to exhibit shorter internode length (distance between the leaves) which means that the garden has shorter, stouter plants.

5. The exact genetic make-up of a particular plant is easily preserved. This means that the characteristics of a super-plant or other novel specimen can be continued.

There are also disadvantages to growing clones:

1. All of the plants from a single clone mother yield the same product. There is no variation. Gardeners growing for personal consumption often wish to grow several different varieties.
2. There is no genetic progression. Since no breeding is taking place, the genetic line remains static. There are no surprises and no new finds. Using clones, there is no way of genetically adapting a line to a particular environment.

HOW CLONES ARE MADE

Cuttings are taken from soft green tissue because the drier, woody sections of the plant do not root as easily. Sections taken are 2-5 inches long with several sets of leaves. The cut is made with a very sharp blade which makes a clean, straight cut, rather than a scissor which pinches and injures the tissue. As the cuttings are made they are placed in a bowl filled with lukewarm water to prevent them from drying out.

Once all the cuttings are taken, they are trimmed of their lower leaves, leaving only one or two sets plus the growing tip. This helps to prevent the cutting from being water stressed. If the leaves were left on the cutting, they would create water demands that the stem end, with a limited draw, cannot meet. Any large fan leaves are also removed for the same reason.

Next, the rooting solution is prepared. Liquid type rooting compounds are the best to use because the active ingredients are in solution and are guaranteed to come in contact with the stem. Powders are often scraped off as the cutting is set in place, and drop off when placed in water. Some popular rooting solutions which work well are Olivia's™, Klone Concentrate™, Hormex™ and Wood's™. The solution is used as directed for woody plants.

The trimmed cuttings are placed either in water or a rooting medium such as vermiculite, rockwool or floral foam which has been watered with one quarter strength flowering formula fertilizer solution. At least ¾ inch of stem is inserted in the rooting medium which is be patted down to make sure that the stem is in direct contact with it.

The cuttings growers make are placed in an area of high humidity to limit water stress. Growers often construct a "mini-greenhouse" using plastic wrap placed over the rooting chamber. Some trays come with clear plastic covers to retain moisture. The cover is removed when the plants develop roots. A fine mist spray helps relieve water stress. The clones respond best to a moderate rather than a bright light. Some gardeners light the clone garden using 2 tubes for an area 4 x 2 feet, 10 watts per square foot. Clones being rooted in water do best when the water is changed frequently and aerated using a small pump and an aquarium bubbler. Rooting blocks or medium must be kept well saturated.

The temperature of the medium affects the rooting time of the clones. Cuttings root fastest when the temperature is kept in the low to mid 70's. At lower temperatures the cuttings take longer to root and are more likely to suffer from infections. Growers report the easiest way to keep the cuttings warm is to use a heating cable or heating mat made especially for germinating and rooting plants. These are available at most plant nurseries and are very inexpensive.

Given good conditions, cuttings usually root in one to two weeks. Some varieties are easier to root than others. For instance Big Bud, is notoriously difficult to root. Skunk and Northern lights are much easier to clone.

Chapter 24
PROBLEMS

Every gardener faces some problems with the garden at one time or another. Environmental problems, insects and diseases can create havoc among the plants and often leave the grower stumped.

The best way gardeners have prevented problems has been to carefully examine the garden at least once a week. First a gardener looks at the entire space. Do the plants look healthy and vigorous? Is their color normal and bright? Then the grower examines a few plants closeup. Do they look healthy? Have they grown since the last examination? Do the leaves or any other plant parts show signs of nutrient problems? Taking a photographer's x 4 or x 8 loupe, available at camera stores, the cultivator looks at the leaves of several plants. He asks, "Are there any abnormalities? Any insects or eggs on the undersides?."

The most common problems with plants are not pests. They are over-watering, under-watering and over-fertilization.

When the medium is waterlogged the roots cannot obtain enough oxygen. At the same time, anaerobic bacteria, which are active in oxygen-free environments, attack the roots and produce ammonia. Plant leaves may curl under from lack of oxygen. Waterlogged medium is not usually a problem for hydroponic gardeners but may occur in a some planting mixes. One solution is to water the plant less.

Roots have a harder time drawing water as the medium dries. During the light hours, the need for water is especially acute. If the roots have no moisture, first the bottom leaves and then the entire plant starts to wilt. Water must be added before the leaves die, which can be only a matter of hours. The old myth that water-stressing the plant increases potency is not relevant to indoor cultivation.

Slight chronic overfertilizing can cause the leaves to curl either upward or underneath. Heavy overfertilizing can cause the plant to wilt in a matter of minutes. When the soil medium has a higher concentration of salts (nutrients) than the plant, it draws water from the plant. The only solution growers reported to this problem is to get rid of the excess nutrient by rinsing it out. Once the plant starts to wilt, a few minutes may mean life or death.

THE PESTS

The best way to deal with pests is to prevent them from infecting the garden. A smart gardener never goes to the indoor garden after being in the yard or around outdoor plants. S/he may inadvertantly carry in pests. While they are kept in check naturally outdoors, they have a field day indoors in a much less hostile environment. Healthy plants should be kept away from infected plants and should not be handled after handling infected ones. The pests most likely to infect an indoor garden are mites, white flies and aphids.

MITES

Mites are not insects but arachnids, related to spiders. They are very small and look like small brown, red or black dots on the undersides of leaves. A blemish can be seen on the top side of the leaf where they have been sucking. The infection may not be noticed until after there are 10-50 of these on a leaf. Using a magnifyer they will be noticed walking around on their eight legs when they are not sucking the plant dry. Mites thrive in a dry environment. High humidity and low temperatures slow them down. See illustrations on page 116.

There are two major problems with mites. First, they breed very quickly, every 8-14 days and they like large families. Secondly, they are hard to control. Before budding, a soap dip or the homemade bug killer will knock down the population. Then pyrethrum and soap sprays will keep it low. Growers realize that the idea is not to expect to eliminate them, but to keep the population down so that it does little damage to the crop. Once established, mite predators, which are other mites which feed on their cousins, keep the population totally under control. It may take several introductions to get them started. There are several different species of predator mites, each does best at a slightly different temperature range. Some growers introduce mixed populations, others just one species.

APHIDS

Aphids are oval looking insects about 1/16 of an inch long that come in a rainbow of colors including white, green, red brown and black. They are soft skinned and are often farmed by ants which squeeze them for their

"honeydew" which is a sugar concentrate. Aphids suck on plants looking for protein. The excess sugars are exuded onto plants and these areas become hot spots for fungal and other infections. Aphids breed very quickly, and like warm, dry climates. They are very susceptible to pyrethrum and dry up from soap sprays. The home-made spray a grower developed works wonders against them. See illustrations on page 118.

WHITEFLIES

Whiteflies look just like a housefly except they are only about 1/5-1/10 the size and are all white. They fly around the plants when they are disturbed. Whiteflies are susceptible to pyrethrum, but the best control is with Trichogamma wasps, which get them under control in just a few weeks.

Trichogamma wasps are about ¼ the size of a whitefly and are harmless to humans and pests but not to whiteflies. They parasitize the larger whitefly egg, laying their egg inside it. Once released they fly around and live in the garden but are rarely seen. Until wasps are introduced the aphid population is kept in check using pyrethrum sprays. The wasps are susceptible to sprays so growers do not spray for several days before release. See illustrations on page 119.

Pesticides

In the past few years there have been giant strides made in the development of safe pesticides for indoor use. A few companies produce safe insecticides in aerosol form which release a measured spray periodically. The aerosols use environmentally safe propellants.

Concerned growers never use pesticides which are recommended only for ornamentals. What this really means is that it is NOT RECOMMENDED for food crops. The best pesticides to use are natural ones which have a short life, or simple non-toxic ones which often act by physical or simple chemical rather than biological means. Some growers have found a few safe pesticides which are available at plant and grow stores. They said they helped to eliminate pest problems.

1. Pyrethrum based insecticides and miticides. Pyrethrum is a broad spectrum insecticide produced by the pyrethrum, a flower closely related to the chrysanthemum. It is toxic to cold-blooded animals including fish. Insects and mites are all susceptible. It seems to have no effects on warm-blooded animals and once it is used it quickly loses its activity. Pyrethrum based insecticides usually state that they can be safely used up to the time of harvest.

TODD '90

2. Soap based insecticides and miticides use the ingredients in soap to physically dry out and incapacitate the pests. These sprays usually come in trigger type bottles. After using, the soap residue dries. Then it can be rinsed off the plant. Liquid soaps found in the supermarket such as Ivory™ and Dr. Bronners™ Peppermint or Eucalyptus can also be used. They are usually diluted at the rate of ½ teaspoon per quart of water.

3. Biological controls. Some pests have natural predators which keep them under control. Predatory mites keep mites under control. Whiteflies are easily controlled using the trichogamma wasp, which lays its egg in the fly egg. These wasps are very tiny, do not bite or sting and are non-social, they do not have nests. Once they are released, they are hard to find because they are so small. But they do a great job and are the best control for white flies.

4. A grower's homemade spray which he said works well has the following recipe:

   1 quart water.
   3 ounces strong onion, peeled
   2 ounces fresh garlic
   2 tobacco cigarettes (remove paper)
   ⅛ teaspoon dishwashing detergent
   4 ounces denatured alcohol
   2 tablespoons buttermilk
   1 Teaspoon Dr. Bronners Peppermint soap.

   The onion, garlic, tobacco and water are mixed in a blender until liquified. Then the mash is cooked until simmering. It is cooled to luke warm. Then the soap, detergent, alcohol and buttermilk are added. The liquid is poured through a fine mesh strainer. The plants are sprayed or dipped. Most of the pests hang around the underside of the leaves. Special care is taken to reach mist these sections. The spray is used every two or three days. **Keep out of the reach of children and pets as the nicotine leached from the tobacco is highly toxic.**

Chapter 25
GROWERS BEWARE

The federal government wants to put growers in prison. To accomplish this goal a Draconian set of laws has been enacted which has little relation to justice and makes a mockery of the tradition of law which has developed over the last 800 years. Ordinarily you might find this dull reading, but it may have a tremendous effect upon the lives of people you know.

English common law which extended to America evolved over a thousand years. One of the main protections offered by the law is the writ (right) of habeas corpus. It became part of English law as a result of a peace treaty signed by King Edward The Elder signed in 906. In 904 Aethelwold, his cousin, led the Danes (Viking colonists) in East Anglia and Northumbria to revolt over unjust treatment. Aethelwold fell in battle and Edward agreed to a legal code known as "The Laws of Edward and Guthrum." Among the concerns of the Danish barons which was addressed was the king's habit of imprisonment without cause.

The code was generally adopted as English common law and was reaffirmed by various kings during their reigns, most notably Henry I, (reigned 1100-1135) who promulgated the "Leges Henrici" which set as its goal maintaining the laws of Edward. The concept of limitations on the rights of the crown (read "government") was even more clearly delineated in the Magna Carta, signed by King John.

King John increased taxes to pay for two disastrous wars in which he unsuccessfully attempted to reclaim the lost territories in Normandy. To insure the barons' compliance he forced them to put up hostages to insure good behavior. The barons were not the only ones with grievances. The administration was accused of corruption, nepotism, strong arm tactics, discounting the peoples' wishes and generally lowering the standard of living. He alienated the Church by temporarily placing its finances in lay hands and into the royal treasury.

Finally, tired of the corruption and abuses resulting from absentee management, the barons formed a council. First they had all the local sheriffs swear allegiance to it, rather than to the king. John, realizing he had no choice, agreed to meet the barons. On June 15, 1215 the barons presented him with their demands, known as the Articles of the Barons, which became the basis for the discussions. A more elaborate charter was signed later in the year.

Article 36 of the Magna Carta states, "Nothing shall henceforth be given for a writ of enquiry touching life or limb, but it shall be granted freely and not denied." This reaffirmed common law that a person cannot be placed in custody except for criminal charge, conviction or civil debt. Habeas Corpus literally translated means "produce the body." It commands the custodian to present to the court the prisoner and to show cause why he is imprisoned.

In spite of the promises of earlier kings, later monarchs continually eroded their subjects' rights. This came to a head in 1679 after a few celebrated cases in which King Charles II refused to act on writs by petitioners. Parliament passed the Habeas Corpus Act, sometimes called the Shaftesbury Act, after its chief supporter. Upon presentation of a writ it called for: 1.) The custodian to bring the prisoner to court to show why he is being held. 2.) To allow him to post bail. 3.) No re-imprisonment once a person is set free on a writ. 4.) Speedy trial of discharge from indictment. 5.) No imprisonment in distant or overseas territories.

The idea that there must be a reason why a person is denied liberty led to the concept that to prove a crime you must present a body of evidence. If there is no evidence, there is no crime.

The provisions of the English Magna Carta were written into the Bill of Rights, which are the first 10 Amendments of the Constitution. They are:

Amend. IV - The right of the people to be secure in their persons, houses, papers, and effects, against unreasonable searches and seizures, shall not be violated, and no Warrants shall issue, but upon probable cause, supported by Oath or affirmation, and particularly describing the place to be searched, and the persons or things to be seized.

Amend. V - No person shall be eld to answer for a capital, or otherwise infamous crime, unless on a presentment or indictment of a Grand Jury, except in cases arising in the land or naval forces, or in the Militia, when in actual service in time of War or public danger; nor shall any person be subject to the same offense to be twice put in jeopardy of life and limb; nor shall be compelled in any criminal case to be a witness against himself, nor be deprived of life, liberty, or property without due process of law, nor shall private property be taken for public use, without just compensation.

Amend. VI - In all criminal prosecutions, the accused shall enjoy the right to a speedy and public trial, by an impartial jury of the State and district wherein the crime shall have been committed, which district shall have been previously ascertained by law, and to be informed of the nature and cause of accusation; to be confronted with the witnesses against him; to have compulsory process for obtaining witnesses in his favor, and to have the Assistance of Counsel for his defense.

Amend. VII - In Suits at common law where the value in controversy shall exceed twenty dollars, the right of trial by jury shall be preserved, and no fact tried by jury, shall otherwise be reexamined in any court in the United States, than according to the rules of common law.

Amend. VIII - Excessive bail shall not be required, nor excessive fines imposed, nor cruel and unusual punishments inflicted.

As a result of the experiences of the Civil War, and the realization that all citizens had certain rights, the XIV Amendment was ratified in 1868. The first section reads, "All persons born or naturalized in the United States and subject to the jurisdiction thereof are citizens of the United States and the state in which they reside. No State shall make or enforce any law which shall abridge the privileges or immunities of citizens of the Untied States; nor shall any State deprive any person of life, liberty or property, without due process of law; nor deny to any person within its jurisdiction the equal protection of laws."

Since the 1970's the U.S. government has been creating a new set of crimes based on hearsay and intent rather than actual perpetration. The RICO and CCE laws allow the government to prove a case against an individual with no hard evidence.

To enforce the laws they have developed new ways of interpreting the Bill of Rights. For instance, "use immunity" has been used to gut the Fifth Amendment's protection against self incrimination. Under this law's provisions, which have been upheld by the Supreme Court, your testimony under oath provides you immunity for what you testify. However, the state is allowed to prosecute you if they can build a case without using your testimony to gather the information to prove your crime.

The "good faith exception" to the fourth amendment's protection from search and seizure without probable cause has made a mockery of the provision's intent. Warrants are routinely issued without probable cause allowing informers to use public information to corroborate credibility. (They have 2 kids named X and Y, a white 4 door 68 Falcon. They live in the white house on Extecey St. They have an unusual electric box on the outside, left side of the house.) Just to tip the scales in favor of police misconduct, the courts have held that even if the warrant is bad, the prosecution can use the illegally gathered evidence.

In the 1970's the government instituted a revolutionary new set of laws never seen in this country since the infamous "Alien and Sedition Acts" enacted under John Adams' Administration and repealed soon after. First the conspiracy laws were revamped so that any planning for a criminal act could be prosecuted as a conspiracy. (Two people planning a misdemeanor are committing a felony.) The RICO and CCE Acts have also been used to make mountains out of molehills. RICO stands for "Racketeering Inspired and Corrupt Organizations," CCE stands for "Continuing Criminal Enterprise."

When these laws were under consideration the proponents claimed that they would be used to clean up the "Mafia" or "Cosa Nostra". However, since their enactment, they have been used to fill federal prisons with unfortunate schnooks. All that is required to fall victim to these statutes is for the prosecution to prove you were involved in two related criminal acts. (Two sales of dime bags?) The conspiracy, RICO, and CCE laws have created a whole new class of criminal who the government just wanted to nail.

The various crime bills created the Federal Sentencing Guideline Commission which was to set up uniform sentencing guidelines. The purpose was to give the courts less discretion in handing out sentences. The commission has been a prosecutor's dream. Regular Joes are regularly slapped with 5-10 year sentences as their property is confiscated and their dependents thrown out on the street.

In 1989 the Federal Sentencing Commission announced new guidelines to implement the laws of the Omnibus Crime Control Act. These guidelines determine the sentences for various crimes. The sentencing level is determined by the quantity of marijuana seized by the government.

Here are the basic levels for marijuana:

SENTENCING GUIDELINES

LEVEL	POT WEIGHT	HASH WEIGHT	HASH OIL WEIGHT
Level 42	300,000 Kg	60,000 Kg	6,000 Kg
Level 40	100,0000-300,000 Kg	20,000-60,000 Kg	20,000-6,000 Kg
Level 38	30,000-100,000 Kg	6,000-20,000 Kg	600-2000 Kg
Level 36	10,000-30,000 Kg	2,000-6,000 Kg	200-600 kg
Level 34	3,000-10,000 Kg	600-2,000 Kg	60-200 Kg
Level 32	1,000-3,000 Kg	200-600 Kg	20-60 Kg
Level 30	700-1000 Kg	140-200 Kg	14-20 Kg
Level 28	400-700 Kg	80-140 Kg	8-14 Kg
Level 26	100-400 Kg	20-80 Kg	2-8 Kg
Level 24	80-100 Kg	16-20 Kg	1.6-2 Kg
Level 22	60-80 Kg	12-16 Kg	1.2-1.6 Kg
Level 20	40-60 Kg	8-12 Kg	800 gm-1.2 Kg
Level 18	20-40 Kg	5-8 Kg	500-800 gm
Level 16	10-20 Kg	2-5 Kg	200-500 gm
Level 14	5-10 Kg	1-2 Kg	100-200 gm
Level 12	2.5-5 Kg	500 gm-1 Kg	50-100 gm
Level 10	1-2.5 Kg	200-500 gm	20-50 gm
Level 8	250 gm-1 Kg	50-200 gm	5-20 gm
Level 6	Less than 250 gm	Less than 50 gm	Less than 5 gm

Besides the basic levels for possession, extra points are given for growing on federal property, using boobytraps, carrying firearms, leadership of an organized group, and a myriad of other violations.

Once the level is determined, the judge refers to the Sentencing Table. For each Level there are six different sentencing tables. The most lenient Table, one, is for victims with a previously clean slate, who would otherwise be considered credits to the community including job and stability. Table six, the harshest, is for the "unredeemable," who have had previous bouts with the drug laws and are considered scum by the courts. Most drug convicts fall somewhere in the middle.

NUMBER OF MONTHS IN FEDERAL PRISON

Level	TABLE 1	TABLE 2	TABLE 3	TABLE 4	TABLE 5	TABLE 6
6	0-6	1-7	2-8	6-12	9-15	12-19
8	2-8	4-10	6-12	10-15	15-21	18-24
10	6-12	8-14	10-16	15-21	21-27	24-30
12	10-16	12-18	15-21	21-27	27-33	30-37
14	15-21	18-24	21-27	27-33	33-41	37-46
16	21-27	4-30	27-33	33-41	41-51	46-57
18	27-33	30-37	33-41	41-51	51-63	57-71
20	33-41	37-46	41-51	51-60	63-70	70-87
22	41-51	46-57	51-63	63-70	77-96	84-110
24	51-63	57-71	63-78	77-96	92-115	100-137
26	63-78	70-87	78-97	92-115	110-137	120-162
28	78-97	87-108	97-121	110-137	130-162	140-152
30	97-121	108-135	121-151	135-168	151-188	168-210
32	121-151	135-168	151-188	168-210	188-235	210-232
34	151-188	168-210	188-235	210-282	235-293	262-327
36	188-235	210-262	235-290	262-327	292-365	324-405
38	235-283	262-327	282-365	324-405	360-LIFE	360-LIFE
40	292-385	324-405	360-LIFE	360-LIFE	360-LIFE	360-LIFE

Now comes the kicker:

"In the case of an offence involving marijuana plants, if the offence involved 50 or more plants, treat each plant as equivalent to 1 Kg of marijuana, lower than 50 marijuana plants, total each plant as equivalent to 100 grams of marijuana. Provided however, that if the actual weight of the marijuana is greater, use the actual weight of the marijuana."

This means someone convicted of cultivating a garden of 140 mature plants and 100 cuttings is considered to be growing 240 kilograms of marijuana, a level 26 and is sentenced to between 63-150 months depending on prior legal history. Although the evidence might weigh less than 3 kilograms, s/he is sentenced as if the person was a large scale grower. A true case of blind justice with a thumb on the scale.

This is a direct violation of the concept of habeas corpus, that the crime charged must fit the body of evidence. By ascribing an arbitrary set weight to the evidence in disregard of its actual weight, the government is discarding one of the prime tenets upon which our laws have evolved for the last 1000 years.

Judges have very little discretion regarding sentencing or humanizing the law. I am familiar with a case in the Pacific Northwest in which small-time growers were convicted under the 1988 guidelines, which considered each plant 100 grams no matter the quantity. They were caught with a garden of mature plants which weighed only 10 grams each. In spite of the evidence the judge declared the law Constitutional and sentenced the drug offender according to the guidelines.

Another section of the law states:

Section 841 1A

Except as otherwise provided in Section 845, 845a or 845b any person who violates subsection (a) shall be sentenced as follows:

(vii) 1000 kilograms or more of a mixture or substance containing a detectable amount of marijuana, or 1000 or more marijuana plants regardless of weight; such person shall be sentenced to a term of imprisonment which may not be less than 10 years or more than life and if death or serious bodily injury results from the use of such substance the term shall not be less than 20 years or more than life, a fine not to exceed $4,000,000. If a person commits such a violation after a prior conviction of a felony drug offense has become final, the person shall be sentenced to a minimum of 20 years and not more than life and if death or serious bodily injury results from the use of the substance, shall be sentenced to life imprisonment.

If a person commits an offence after two or more prior convictions for a felony drug offense have become final the person shall be sentenced to mandatory life imprisonment.

(vii) 100 kilograms or more of a mixture containing marijuana or 100 or more marijuana plants regardless of weight. Such a person shall be sentenced to a term of imprisonment not less than 5 years or more than 40. 20 years if death or serious bodily injury occurs, and a fine of up to $2,000,000. With a single prior drug felony: 10 years.

In the case of less than 50 kilograms of marijuana, except in the case of 50 or more marijuana plants regardless of weight or 10 kilograms of hashish or one kilogram of hash oil such person shall be sentenced to imprisonment for no more than 5 years and a fine of no more than $250,000. If the person has a prior drug conviction, the term of imprisonment shall be no more than 10 years.

Under the federal system only 15% of the sentence can be mitigated for good behavior. A person sentenced to 10 years in prison serves a minimum of 8 1/2 years.

Most people are not aware how harsh the marijuana laws are. I recently read a column written by Jack Anderson about the plight of an

American sentenced to death in Malaysia for a pound of pot. Mr. Anderson and other opinion molders are apparently unaware of the living death sentences faced by American marijuana users.

Perhaps we can educate the media about the terrible impact these laws are having on American lives: that the simple pleasure of "growing your own" can cost you 5-10 years of your life plus your life savings. Send copies of these guidelines to newspapers and other media with your letters to let them know just how medieval the American court system is. Also send letters to the three organizations demanding that they take action to petition the Federal Sentencing Guidelines Committee to change policies regarding marijuana cultivation. They are:

Don Fiedler
NORML LEGAL COMMITTEE
1636 R St. NW
Washington, D.C. 20009

Kevin Zeese
DRUG POLICY FOUNDATION
4801 Massachusetts Ave. NW
Washington, D.C. 20016

Keith Stroup
NATIONAL ASSOCIATION OF CRIMINAL DEFENSE LAWYERS
1110 Vermont Ave.
Washington D.C.20005

These organizations are on our side but they need to get stirred up on this issue which affects so many people.

One attorney who works with the Commission told me that public opinion may also affect their decisions. Letters should be addressed to:

Chairman William Wilkins
Federal Sentencing Guidelines Commission
1331 Pennsylvania Avenue, NW
Washington, D.C. 20004

Tell them the reality of growing, and how much a plant yields. Also tell them how unfair the guidelines are. Tell them that their sentencing structure is more damaging to both the individual and society than what they are trying to protect society from. The DEA's own Administrative Law Judge, Judge Young, has ruled that marijuana should be reclassified so it can be used medically. In his ruling he said that marijuana was one of the most benign medicines known to man. Tell them about the non-medical uses of marijuana. And tell them that a six year sentence for a closet garden is a cruel and unusual punishment.

A NEW HORTICULTURE BOOK FROM
LAST GASP

The CLOSET CULTIVATOR

by Ed Rosenthal

A new easy-to-handle book written by the foremost expert of cannabis cultivation is a fountain of detailed information on the various factors that influence the growth and development of hemp. It explains in clear language how growers control their plantations in a way applicable to most vegetable growth. We know that this book will be truly appreciated by the readers who made best sellers of the other books on this page.

A LAST GASP BEST SELLER

The SINSEMILLA TECHNIQUE

A steady seller for the past ten years, this book was the first one to present the agricultural entrepreneurs of California's Emerald Belt to the public at large. It tells of family farms, friendly communities and hassle-free lives before greed and the Law invaded Northern California. 6th printing. SINTEC $19.95

The BEST INFORMATION

The MOST RECENT TECHNIQUES

The BEST SELLING HORTICULTURE BOOK Year after Year after Year.

MARIJUANA GROWER'S GUIDE DELUXE

by Ed Rosenthal & Mel Frank

First published in 1978, now in its 25th printing and constantly updated to reflect the advances of the art., this is THE reference book for anyone interested in whichever quality by the cultivation of Cannabis. MARGRD $19.95

SEND TO:
LAST GASP OF
SAN FRANCISCO
777 FLORIDA STREET
SAN FRANCISCO,
CALIFORNIA 94110
(415) 824-6636

METHOD OF PAYMENT (US Funds Only):
( ) Check
( ) Money Order
( ) VISA
( ) MASTERCARD

ORDER FORM

	INCLUDES SHIPPING & HANDLING	
CLOSET CULTIVATOR	$20.00	
MARIJUANA GROWERS GUIDE	$25.00	
SINSEMILLA TECHNIQUE	$25.00	

Cardholder's name: ______________________

Card # ☐☐☐☐ ☐☐☐☐ ☐☐☐☐ ☐☐☐☐

Expiration Date: ______________________

Authorized Signature: ______________________

I hereby certify that I am 18 or older:

Signature: ______________________

Total costs of books	
Total Amount - Enclose Payment	

ALLOW 4 TO 6 WEEKS FOR DELIVERY

PRICES SUBJECT TO CHANGE WITHOUT WARNING